KAY KUZMA

creating

Love

Principles that will
revolutionize your relationships
and turn obnoxious people
into lovable ones

Pacific Press® Publishing Association
Nampa, Idaho
Oshawa, Ontario, Canada

Edited by Kenneth R. Wade
Cover photos ©1996 Adobe Systems Incorporated
Cover and inside design by Michelle C. Petz

Unless otherwise specified, Bible texts used are from the New King James Version.

Accuracy of all quotations and references is the responsibility of the author.

Kuzma, Kay.
　　Creating love : principles that can revolutionize your relation-
ships and turn obnoxious people into lovable ones / Kay Kuzma.
　　　　p.　cm.
　　ISBN 0-8163-1382-2 (pbk. : alk. paper)
　　　　1. Love—Religious aspects—Christianity.　2.　Christian life—
Seventh-day Adventist authors.　I. Title.
　　BV4639.K89　1997
241'.4—dc21　　　　　　　　　　　　　　　　96-47976
　　　　　　　　　　　　　　　　　　　　　　　　CIP

98 99 00 01 • 5 4 3 2

This book is dedicated
to those who are longing for love:

- to the young who are alive with the newness of romance and are anticipating a lifetime commitment with their beloved.
- to the couple who have celebrated the intimacy of oneness and desire to keep their hearts ablaze with the mystery of love.
- and to those who have awakened to the reality that love takes time, touch, and toughness.
- to those who have once found love and now sorrow in their incredible loss.
- to you who are suffering from cups cracked by abuse and seeking the glue of God's love that makes a life worth living.

And with a thankful heart to God
who has given me my heart's desire,
I dedicate this book to my husband, Jan,
who has been my lifetime
love partner and cup filler.

Contents

Preface

Have you ever yearned for some magic to turn your life around? Something to heal your aching heart, restore hope and confidence, spark creativity, motivate you to service, free you from tyranny, and somehow transform the unloved into the beloved?

Who wouldn't welcome such a miracle! You might be willing to pay a high price for its formula. But you don't have to. It's available to everyone free.

What is this miracle? Love. I didn't invent it. But I'm fortunate to have experienced it. And I've discovered that nothing else in the world has the life-changing power love has.

Are you looking for romance to brighten up a dull life? Romance will never fill you with complete satisfaction, unless its foundation is the kind of love expressed in 1 Corinthians 13, that is patient and kind and not envious, boastful, proud, rude, selfish, or easily angered. You want a love that keeps no record of wrongs and doesn't delight in evil but rejoices with the truth. And one that always protects, trusts, hopes, perseveres, and never fails. An impossible dream? No, not when you discover the love-cup principle.

Are you thinking about starting a family? Don't unless

you have made the love cup your philosophy of life. Child-birth classes may prepare you for a less-painful birth and allow Dad to ceremoniously cut the umbilical cord, but they won't insure painless child-rearing.

If you are a parent or a grandparent and have picked up the erroneous idea that children should be treated as they deserve to be treated, you've probably discovered the painful fact that "fairness" doesn't work. Why? What a child deserves is not necessarily what he or she needs. Effective child-rearing means meeting children's needs, and their greatest need is to be loved irrationally—regardless of what they do or what they deserve.

Maybe you're struggling to fulfill your Master's commission to "love your enemies" or "to love others as God loves you," and you just don't know how to do it. The love-cup principle will make the abstract concept of love so concrete and practical that you'll be overflowing with ideas.

No one is too young or too old not to benefit from the love-cup principle, either as a recipient or as a giver. And the beauty of it all is that the love cup offers an abundant, unending supply of love, for when you give it away, it has a way of coming back. Love creates love.

This is a book for everyone who has ever desired to give love—or receive it. And it's a book you'll want to review throughout the stages of your life, because love should never end, and it won't if you keep filling the love cup.

> "To love is to place our happiness
> in the happiness of another."
> —*Gottfried Wilhelm Von Leibnitz*

Acknowledgments

To Elmar Sakala, my friend and colleague at Loma Linda University, this book is partly yours, for the kernel was formed as we taught Family Health together.

And to the people along my way who have filled my love cup and encouraged a broader ministry—Dan Matthews, for urging me to move forward with radio; Roy Naden, who made it happen; Lee McIntyre, with whom I first recorded; and a special thanks to Jon Fugler and Rees Evans, who have worked with me for over a decade, molding and producing radio programming to encourage and inspire parents to give their best to their children. But most of all to Edwin and Mary Belle Martin, whose vision and generosity brought us to our beautiful Tennessee home on a wooded hill overlooking the Smokies: "a place where I could write." Their unselfish gift of giving to others what God has given to them has inspired me to care and share more abundantly.

And to my family and friends, I love you.

"Ah, my beloved, fill the cup that clears
Today of past regrets and future fears."
—*Omar Khayyam*

Chapter One

How Love Creates Love

"Life's richest cup is love's to fill—
Who drinks, if deep the draught shall be,
Knows all the rapture of the hill
Blent with the heartbeat of the sea."
—*Robert Cameron Rogers*

Down deep in your heart there's a cup. Not of fine china, silver, or gold. But a cup of feeling and emotion, that when filled makes life worth living. I call it the love cup. It measures your level of contentment. In essence, it's your psychological well-being.

To speak of a cup of love is, of course, a metaphor. But this word picture might help you better understand a difficult concept.

Creating Love

Let me see if I can't help get you in touch with your cup. Close your eyes. Picture yourself as a child, snuggled close to your mom's sweet scent of lilac. She's rocking you. She smiles; you smile. She strokes your cheek. Softly, she sings a lullaby. Your tummy is full of her good milk. You're warm and cozy and dry. Do you feel yourself filling? Ahh, such contentment!

You're in school—your favorite teacher pauses at your desk, gently touches you arm, smiles, and says, "Do you have any idea how lucky I feel to be your teacher? You're doing so well in your schoolwork. And I appreciate how kind and helpful you are to your classmates. Thank you for being you." Are you catching the feeling?

Pause again, and think of a warm spring day. The scent of blossoms in the air, birds singing. No clocks. No worries. Picture yourself with someone you really care about, someone you love. You feel secure next to this person. It just feels good being close. Then that special one turns to you, gives you a hug, and shares how much you're appreciated—how much your friendship means.

Concentrate on the scene for a few seconds. Wow, how do you feel? What's happening to your love cup? Can you feel it filling? Surely you do; love transforms, motivates, and inspires.

It's not a romantic love, of which I write. Passion is a roller-coaster dependent on circumstances: driven by desire; stimulated by physical involvement, and depressed by hurt and alienation. The love that fills the empty place in a heart is neither *eros*, nor *philos*—a love that gives to get. It is *agape*. It is a principle, not necessarily devoid of emotion, but not dependent on it either. It is love given with no strings attached, just because the other exists. When experienced, endorphins—which are chemically similar to morphine—flow into the brain, producing the sense of security, peace, and calm. One feels good because one feels intrinsically valuable.

Much of the time we're unaware of the cup within us. We get by, existing from day to day with a partly filled cup. When it's empty, we feel it hard and cold within, almost like we're dying. When it's full, we feel the other extreme, an all-encompassing warmth and contentment. It makes us eager to share. We want to sing and shout for joy, and we truly begin to live.

Life is for living, not merely existing. No one wants to falter from an insufficient love supply. So think about that love cup inside you. Sharpen your senses to signal you when your cup begins to empty. Fine-tune your perceptions to the feelings of others. Learn to catch their signal, "my love cup is running low."

Your love cup and behavior

Your love cup is like an emotional barometer that can predict behavior. When it's full and overflowing, you become a loving person. It's as if your life is so filled with love that you can't hold it all! You want to share those good feelings with others. But when your cup is running low, you feel unloved, rejected, worthless, and empty—you have nothing to give. When your cup is drained, your world turns negative: anger, criticism, sarcasm, guilt, and bitterness rush in to fill the void. You have nothing but bitter gall to share with others.

Most children and many adults equate love with attention. When denied attention they feel unloved. So they seek attention. And it doesn't take long for a child to learn a sure-fire road to get it: just be obnoxious, disobedient, or destructive! Many grow up viewing life negatively—becoming bossy, demanding, sarcastic, demeaning, or complaining individuals. They blame God for dealing them a losing hand. They are unhappy, perhaps bitter, because their fathers never gave moral support, or their mothers failed to comfort them, or their friends wouldn't stand up for them. They live in an alien world where no one cares. Fearful of being taken advantage of and hurt once again, they've learned to look out for themselves. They spend their time selfishly indulging themselves, too often stepping on others to get what they want. But what they really want—love—seems always to elude them.

They never experience the joy of giving; they never feel they have anything to give. Their lives are empty; they crave love. But their love cups remain empty because they have never learned the lesson, "It is more blessed to give than to receive." They don't appreciate the fact that the more you give the more you will receive. In their overwhelming concern for themselves, they develop characteristics that make them difficult to live with and nearly impossible to love.

Mindy's husband was difficult to love. He never remembered his dad saying, "I love you," and he grew up having to look out for himself. Now married, he found it hard to be warm and responsive. Mindy was just about ready to give up on her marriage when she came to the weekend women's retreat and heard these words, "Do you sometimes feel empty and wish someone would give you a little love and attention? Well, the answer might be to first give some love away." Mindy was intrigued by the love-cup principle. Could it be that her husband was unloving because his love cup was empty and he had nothing to give? She determined to try and fill him up. Then when he was full and overflowing there might be a chance that he could be loving too.

Mindy decided to make a list of all the reasons she loved her husband. When she got home from the retreat she asked him to sit down because she had a list of things to read him. His back bristled. Immediately he thought about the faucet that didn't work and the light bulb that needed changing. He sat in silence as Mindy began reading her list, absorbing words he hadn't heard since honeymoon days. At the end, he smiled weakly and asked, "Is that all?"

"Oh no," she said quickly, thinking of a few more reasons.

He then got up and went to his desk and shuffled through some papers. Nothing like this had occurred in their marriage for a long time, and he just didn't know how to respond.

Now I must interrupt and give you an insight that happened a number of years before. Then I'll tell you the end of the story. Mindy had wanted a mixer that kneaded bread dough. She knew the budget could never stand this luxury item, but she asked her husband anyway. "Honey, do you think we could get one of those mixers that makes bread?"

"I'll make a deal with you," he bargained, "if you lose weight, I'll get you a mixer." Mindy tried. She starved herself and gained five pounds. Two years went by. No weight lost—and no mixer. And then the love list.

Later that afternoon he called to Mindy. "Oh, Mindy, I've decided I should go down to the bank and arrange for the financing to get the jeep fixed, and while I'm there I might as well get enough money for that bread mixer that you've been wanting." It was his way of saying, "Mindy, I love you too."

And the result? Mindy began losing weight—even with

mouth-watering loaves of fresh home-baked bread in the kitchen!

What can you learn from Mindy's story? Just this. When you feel unloved and your life seems empty, it's time to start reaching out to others. But in the process of filling others with love, the chances are that love will be poured back into your life in ways that you might least expect.

But caution! Don't give love to get! Give love because God says that's what you should do. Give love regardless of the outcome. Give love even though it may seem wasted.

Love-cup control

I was lecturing to graduate students and mentioned the love-cup principle. One of my students told her little five-year-old about it when he came to her complaining that his little two-year-old sister, Missy, was being mean to him. Missy was a very demanding child and was often a miserable playmate. Mom took a few minutes to explain that when people get mean and miserable, it just might be that their love cups are empty. She then challenged him to see if he could find a way to fill Missy's love cup. A few minutes later she heard him say, "Missy, would you like to color in my new coloring book with my new crayons?" Mom couldn't believe it. He was offering his prized possession to his sister, and for the next two hours they played happily together.

That evening after supper, Mom went back to the bedroom to study while Dad cleaned up the supper dishes. Something must have happened, because Dad said some angry words to their son and a few minutes later Junior tramped into the room where Mom was studying, saying, "Daddy's emptying my love cup."

"Well, remember what I told you this morning," said

Mom. "Whenever someone gets upset and says things he shouldn't it's probably because of an empty love cup."

"You mean Daddy has a love cup too?" the child asked in surprise.

A few minutes later Mom heard this boy say, "Daddy, I love you. And can I help you with the dishes?"

The next week when graduate-student Mom came back to class she greeted me with, "Dr. Kay, you'll never believe what's happened in our family. Our five-year-old has total control!

"What?" I exclaimed.

"Yes," she stated, "Whenever we get upset and say something we shouldn't, he fills our love cups and we have to change."

I'm really not for children controlling the family—unless it's love-cup control. And then, the more the better!

The original love cup

He was sitting alone beside the well. His friends had gone to the city to get something to eat, and He expected them back momentarily. And then He saw her approaching. He knew immediately who she was—a woman who had been married to five men and was working on the sixth! Certainly she was not the type of woman any respectable man would want to get caught alone with—especially since He was Jewish, and she was Samaritan. Any other man would have hidden behind a palm tree and prayed that she would get her water quickly and leave before his presence was detected. But not Jesus. He knew she came to the well with more than an empty bucket. Her love cup was empty and she was desperately trying to fill it herself. Why else had she gone through so many men?

She must have been startled to find someone at the well. Most came in the early morning or evening. Why was she coming at noon? Probably trying to avoid those who would criticize her lifestyle or pretend she didn't exist.

Then He asked for a drink. If He had offered help, she would have refused, knowing she was unworthy. But suddenly the tables were turned. He took the role of the helpless. It made her feel valuable to realize she could do something to help.

And then the simple conversation about how her life could be so filled that she would never feel empty again—and she perceived that this man was no ordinary person. He didn't treat her as she deserved to be treated. But instead, He gave her what she so desperately needed—some positive attention. And her cup filled with love. No man had ever treated her like this before. And she raced back to town announcing, " I have met the Messiah!"

Aren't you glad Jesus never treats us as we deserve to be treated—only as we need to be treated. He loved us first. He doesn't say, "Shape up and then I'll fill you to overflowing." He just fills, if we'll let Him, and our lives change accordingly.

God can enter a life that's filled with hate and selfishness. He can change it. In a sense, that's the meaning of conversion. No one is beyond God's healing power to love. But just because God can do it doesn't mean we should leave the filling entirely to Him. God gives us the opportunity to be His entering wedge. When people are starved for love, they may first need to experience a little love in action; next they come to the realization that their lives are empty. Then they can be pointed to the Source.

If you feel empty, ask God to fill you. He will speedily

respond, and send out others who can be cup fillers too. Then when your cup is filling, or full, reach out and begin filling the empty love cups of the unlovable. You may not feel loving, but that doesn't matter, God asks no one to *feel loving*. He just says, *be loving*. It's the act of love that is important. Love is something you do. And as you love, both you and the one whose cup you are filling will begin to live life abundantly!

Chapter Two

Don't Empty a Love Cup

"There are moments in life,
when the heart is so full of emotion,
That if by chance it be shaken,
or into its depths like a pebble
Drops some careless word,
it overflows, and its secret,
Spilt on the ground like water,
can never be gathered together."
—*Henry Wadsworth Longfellow*

Without positive attention the love in a cup will slowly evaporate. It needs constant replenishment to stay full to the brim. So the best way to make sure that a love cup is as full as possible is deceptively simple: don't neglect it, don't deliberately empty it, and by all means, don't crack it!

Although cup emptying can happen at any age, the major at-risk population is dependent children, because they have little or no choice concerning their environments. But beware, the same cup-emptying techniques are at work destroying relationships between husbands and wives, grown children and their parents, and among friends, church members, and coworkers. If you find yourself in a situation where cups are being emptied, do something about it. Cup-emptying abuse must be stopped!

Don't neglect the love cup!

Sometimes a love cup is emptied, not because of overt cup emptying, but merely because no one cared enough to fill it. A sin of omission.

Joyce came to one of my seminars. I talked about the ten traits of strong, healthy families based on the summary of a number of research studies. In rank order the ten are:

> 1: Commitment
> 2: Appreciation and affirmation
> 3: Time together
> 4: Communication
> 5: Shared religious belief
> 6: Play and a sense of humor
> 7: Shared goals and interests
> 8: Flexible roles meeting family needs
> 9: Service to others
> 10: Willingness to solve problems

After hearing the list, Joyce was in tears. "I missed childhood!" she sobbed. She then went on to weave a tale of woe

Creating Love

that basically pointed out that her family of origin did not give her any of the ten traits necessary for meaningful family life and psychological health. Her story went something like this: "My folks were never home, and finally Dad ran off with another woman and I never heard from him again. My mom believed that if she said anything good about me I'd become proud or conceited, so I never heard a word of appreciation from her lips, even though I craved her approval and worked for it all my life. We didn't talk to each other. The TV was my companion. It blared morning, noon, and night. And when my folks needed to tell me something, they shouted commands. Mom never asked my opinion. She demanded exact obedience. To me God was just as far away psychologically as my father. I had no idea that God loved me or wanted my friendship, and my family never went anywhere together—certainly not to church. There was no play in our home, just work, work, work. Life was serious business. Few of my needs were met. I got up by myself, got my breakfast, got dressed, got off to school, got supper, entertained myself, and went to bed, many days without even seeing my folks. We didn't have close relatives or family friends, and I had no example of selfless living—reaching out and helping others. Life was hopeless. There was never a plan to solve problems. We merely existed."

How many grow up in this world, empty by omission, products of men and women with no sense of commitment to each other, let alone commitment to the children they bring into the world? I'm frightened when I think about the magnitude of the problem.

Empty people. It's more than a song that brings tears to your eyes. It's real. And our answer to the problem? If a family of origin can't be salvaged, are there truly not enough foster care or adoptive homes for these children? They say foster care placement is drying up as potential care-giving mothers leave the home for higher-paying jobs. They say there is not enough welfare money for teen mothers who keep having babies. Orphanages? That can't be the answer! My mind jogs back to the horror stories after World War I when orphanages were overflowing with parentless children. Why did so many of these children not sit up until after one year of age? Why did so many not walk until after two? Why did so many die during those first few years? They had enough food, safe shelter, a crib. It was the sin of omission. Staff served in shifts. There were too many mouths to feed; too many bottoms to diaper. And no one with the time, energy, or inclination to love.

Omission isn't just a poverty problem. I taught at UCLA's prestigious elementary school where parents enrolled their children the moment they were born and hoped there would be a place for them by the time they were preschoolers. Those families were willing to pay any amount for this privilege. Money was no problem. I'll never forget one girl I'll call Shelly. She came to school reeking of urine. A number of times when the other children complained too vehemently that they didn't want to sit next to Shelly because, "She stinks!" I took her into the restroom, gave her a sponge bath, shampooed her tangled hair, and changed her into some extra clothing we kept on hand. Shelly's parents? He was a full professor at the university. Her mother was a socialite. Yet Shelly was a deprived child! Deprived of parental love and care. When I spoke to her mother, she blamed the maid. I never saw the maid, but I know one thing: Shelly was neither the parents' nor the maid's priority!

Omission, to have an emptying effect, does not need to

be as blatantly neglectful as the stories I've related. A child can grow up empty with folks who care for their basic physical needs, but just don't realize that children also need an abundance of encouragement, approval, praise, and appreciation to grow to maturity psychologically healthy.

Some folks, themselves the products of parents who were overly involved in commitments outside the home, don't realize the importance of shooting baskets with the kids, of picnics in the park, of wrestling on the floor, or of bedtime stories. For healthy growth, children need the psychological involvement of their parents. They need to feel they are important to their folks. When job, problems, or TV addiction steal the time that rightfully belongs to growing children and teenagers, that's abusive.

Look again at the list of traits that make families healthy and strong. These are the same traits that are essential for children to grow up with intact love cups, filled and overflowing. If there is a trait that's missing in your family, don't waste your time blaming your parents, a working wife, a traveling husband, or the government. Take immediate steps to fill the gap. Don't be guilty of cup emptying by omission!

Love, like water, evaporates over time if not replenished. Daily living with the stress and strain of social acceptance, school achievement, and job success, tends to absorb more psychological energy than you might think from both young and old.

Love is something like vitamins. People can probably get all the essential vitamins they need if they eat a nutritionally balanced diet. But just in case, it never hurts to take a daily multi-vitamin capsule. The same with love—it never hurts to give a little extra, just to make sure cups stay full.

What's the daily dose that will assure a psychologically healthy love cup? I'd prescribe a little extra:

- Vitamin A: *Attention* that is positive and focused— at least fifteen minutes each day.
- Vitamin B: *Bear hugs* each morning and evening.
- Vitamin C: *Compliments* throughout the day.
- Vitamin D: *Discipline* to learn how to fill other love cups.
- Vitamin E: *Encouragement* as often as needed, which is the vitamin that is especially good for the heart!

Don't deliberately empty the love cup!

How do you empty a cup? Each time you reject, shame, or humiliate a person, you empty their cup. Here are some of the most common emptying practices.

Bossing. Bossy people finish last in popularity contests. Nobody likes to be pushed around. Naturally, at times everyone needs instruction, but it can be given without ordering and shouting. You don't have to act like a drill sergeant.

Threatening. It's one thing to calmly explain logical consequences; it's another to threaten in order to manipulate the person's behavior. To voice a thought such as a threat, is to increase the likelihood that someday you will carry it out. Don't say what you don't mean.

Pointing out the consequence of certain behavior is instructive. "If you get a ticket for driving too fast, you will have to pay it yourself." That's different from saying, "If you don't quit driving so fast I'll never ride with you again." A threat is an illogical, angry statement given with the intent of forcing the person to conform regardless of whether it makes sense or not. Force empties love cups.

Criticizing. "That was a stupid thing to do. I've never seen such a sloppy job. Look at this messy house. What a pig pen!" Critical words point out faults. Dwelling on weaknesses doesn't start one on the road to improvement. It may be helpful to comment on the situation that disturbs you, but don't criticize the person. Saying, "When things are left on the floor, I'm embarrassed to have friends over," goes over a lot better than calling a person stupid or insinuating that the person is a pig because he or she lives in a mess! Instead of saying, "What a stupid thing to do," simply point out what the person should have done, "Next time, consider the consequences first."

Ridicule and sarcasm are especially offensive ways of criticizing. Ridicule doesn't correct behavior, it humiliates and demeans people into feelings of worthlessness. When a person feels that way it's quite difficult to change for the better. It takes much courage and a high feeling of self-worth to say, "I can change." That's why put-downs are so devastating.

Screaming. Being screamed at has a way of making us shrink to midget size. A high-pitched, out-of-control voice—no matter the words—makes one cower. Scream, "I love you," to a dog and watch him drop his tail between his legs and slink off to a corner. The tone of voice we use when speaking to others can either empty or fill their love cups.

Rejecting. People feel the sting of rejection when friends or loved ones blurt out their angry feelings: "Leave me alone." But being ignored can be just as painful. That's why it's so important to remember special days, choose to spend time together, and in little ways let the other know you care, even if you're not there.

Being so busy that your children are lost in the shuffle makes them feel rejected. You fail in those regular love routines: the goodnight story, the piggy-back ride. Or unthinkingly when your child asks to do something special with you or needs your help, you snap, "No."

Children feel rejection when their parents don't spend time with them. A divorce, a condo across town, and every other weekend isn't the child's idea of what parents are for—and physical absence can easily be perceived as rejection, especially if Dad (or Mom) never calls during the week and gets a baby sitter while the kids are "visiting."

But being physically present yet psychologically absent hurts even more. Don't let work and worry invade the precious present and destroy your family time. Give the kids your full attention, fill them up, and their joy and contentment will splash back on you! (And while you're at it, splash a little on your spouse, as well!)

Ask any grandparent, "What would you do differently if you were given a second chance to raise your children?" and I can almost guarantee the answer. "I wouldn't be so harsh. I'd spend more time with them." A grandmother once commented, "One day you're diapering them and the next day they're gone. If I could do it again, I'd even enjoy the dirty diapers!"

Parents are people too. They need privacy at times. Tell your children you need a quiet hour alone. They'll usually respect that without feeling rejected. They can understand when you need to cool off. Say, "I'm so angry, I'm about to explode. Give me fifteen minutes alone." They'll probably say, "Take thirty if you need it!" The answer to a little peace and quiet, short of checking in to a local motel, is to fill your family first. They will then be better able to accept your need for privacy.

The years fly quickly. Don't reject or ignore. Give the people in your life the attention—the love—they need to feel filled, today.

Don't crack the love cup!

I hesitate to mention abuse, because none of us wants to consider even the possibility that we might be abusive. But it happens. Too little sleep, too much emotion, too little support, too much pressure and anyone can explode, acting irrationally—battering physically or psychologically. The result can be life damaging: a cracked love cup.

You've met people with cracked love cups. These are individuals who regardless of how much filling you do, never fill up. All your positive attention just seems to leak out the cracks. You try to compliment, you do nice things for them, you invite them to dinner, you send cards to celebrate their birthdays, but there is never enough love. They never are able to fill to the overflowing level where they can experience contentment and generously give love in return.

It's tiring to keep filling. But God didn't command us to just fill those who have intact love cups. He just said, "Love others as I have loved you." Never love to get love in return. Regardless of the response, we must keep filling.

It is not our responsibility to fix cracked cups. If you are instrumental in someone's healing, praise the Lord. But in most cases professional help is required to repair the damage inflicted on a person who has suffered physical, mental, or sexual abuse. Often human healing is merely a patch job on the outside of the cup, and in times of crisis leakage once more occurs. Sometimes it's only God's Holy Spirit who can give the true gift of healing, putting a protective coating of His love on the inside of their cups, as they realize for the first time that God loves them unconditionally and that regardless of what has happened in their past, they are valuable.

In attempting to fix others' cups, there is a danger that you can become an enabler. Enablers are people who get their feelings of significance by protecting people from the consequences of their own destructive behavior, taking responsibility for others' lives that they should carry themselves.

Since cracked cups are difficult to heal, you must put your energy into preventing cracked cups. You must stop abuse! If you're in an abusive relationship, you must take steps to protect yourself and/or your children. God values you. It is not His desire that any of His royal children, regardless of age, should ever be mistreated.

Never forget, a love cup is easy to empty. So when people around you act unlovely, don't treat them as you may feel they deserve—bossing, threatening, criticizing, screaming, or rejecting. If you do these things, you may end up depleting an already meager love supply and make the situation worse. Instead, try filling their love cups. You'll be surprised what a difference it makes!

Chapter Three

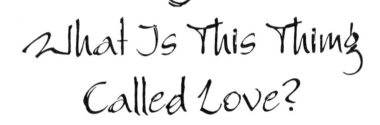

What Is This Thing Called Love?

"What is this thing called love?
What? Is this thing called love?
What is this thing called? Love?
However punctuated,
Cole Porter's simple question begs an answer."
—*Paul Gray*

Love is the critical ingredient for transforming children into loving adults, for changing unlovable grownups into lovable ones. But what is this powerful something? What exactly is love?

In a broad sense, love is giving—giving of oneself to another without the expectation of receiving anything in return. The opposite is selfishness—thinking more of yourself than of others; meeting your needs ahead of others'; taking and not giving; giving and expecting reciprocation.

In essence, love is patient and kind, not envious or jealous, not conceited or proud; it is not ill-mannered or irritable; it forgives and forgets; it detests wrongdoing and is happy about the truth. It believes in others and is optimistic. It is longsuffering and will last forever. At least that's the definition of love the apostle Paul gives.

Without looking back at the last paragraph could you recite the fifteen characteristics of love found in 1 Corinthians 13? Probably not. Here's the list again:

1. Patient and longsuffering
2. Kind and thoughtful
3. Not envious or jealous
4. Not boastful or proud
5. Not rude, ill-mannered, or irritable
6. Not selfish
7. Not easily angered
8. Keeps no record of wrongs—forgives and forgets
9. Doesn't delight in evil—detests wrongdoing
10. Rejoices or is happy with the truth
11. Always protects
12. Always trusts
13. Always hopes and is optimistic about the future
14. Always perseveres regardless of problems and difficulties
15. And never fails

It's a long list and tough to remember. Yet, it's important to be aware of the components of love in order to keep your child's, your mate's, or your friend's love cup full. Here is an easier way—just remember five characteristics: care, respect, acceptance, forgiveness, and trust; for all the others are contained within these five. Let the acronym CRAFT be your working definition of love: C for *Care*, R for *Respect*, A for *Acceptance*, F for *Forgiveness*, and T for *Trust*.

Here's how the fifteen characteristics of love in 1 Corinthians 13 can be categorized under CRAFT:

CARE
  Patient and long-suffering
  Kind and thoughtful
  Not selfish
  Rejoices or is happy with the truth
RESPECT
  Not boastful or proud
  Not rude, ill-mannered, or irritable
ACCEPTANCE
  Always perseveres regardless of problems and difficulties
  Never fails
FORGIVENESS
  Keeps no record of wrongs—forgives and forgets
TRUST
  Not envious or jealous
  Always protects
  Always trusts
  Always hopes and is optimistic about the future

When you ask yourself, "Was that a loving thing to do?," check your behavior with CRAFT, and you'll have an immediate answer. Ask, "Did I *care* for the other's needs? "Did I show *respect*?" "Was I *accepting*?" "Have I shown a spirit of *forgiveness*?" "Am I worthy of *trust*?"

C = Care

Would babies really feel loved if you cooed, "I love you," but never fed them when hungry, diapered them when wet, or held them when they cried? Hardly. They might be lulled to sleep with the cooing, but scientists tell us that to a newborn, the sound of heartbeats may be even more soothing than words. Or would our mates feel loved if we smothered them with things, but were never home to touch, listen to, or share?

Words are wonderful, but if they're not accompanied by caring actions, they become meaningless prattle. Presents are nice, but if they're not accompanied by your presence, they become merely something more to dust or repair.

A primary way to fill a love cup is to put your feelings into practice by caring for the physical and emotional needs of your loved ones. As Erich Fromm wrote in his well-known book, *The Art of Loving*, "Love is an activity; if I love, I am in a constant state of active concern with the loved person."

Care is love in action. Attitude plus behavior. It's reaching out to the helpless, the down and out, those who are in need, no matter how unattractive, sick, or obstinate.

When I think of caring for another's needs, my mind goes to that rocky road between Jerusalem and Jericho. I see this slightly stooped Jewish merchant loaded with wares make his way slowly in the direction of Jericho. Suddenly a couple of punks jump him, bash his face, knock him to the ground, and then kick him. They strip him, grab his bags, money pouch and lunch, and leave him for dead.

What if that Samaritan man would have bent down beside the man and said, "Oh, sir, I'm so sorry about what happened to you. I want you to know that my heart is aching for you and I care so much for you that I'm going to pray for you all day as I go about my business," then stood up and walked away? What would we have called that Samaritan? We certainly wouldn't have called him "good!" Why was he the "Good" Samaritan? Because he didn't just spout words. He put his feelings into action and cared for the man's needs. He took his time to help the man, to take him to an inn and pay for his care. To care for this man took the Good Samaritan's time and money! The Samaritan earned the name "good" because he went beyond kindness in word, to kindness of deed.

How can you be the Good Samaritan to your children, to your mate, to your parents? To your friends and neighbors? When is it your responsibility to care for another's needs?

R = Respect

To respect means to honor and esteem. But there are many who don't deserve it. What then do you do?

It was a busy street. A crowd had gathered around a man they called the Messiah. Among the curiosity seekers was a rather short fellow. Zacchaeus by name. Tax collector by trade. Thief by nature. He started to push through the crowd, but no one would step aside. Not for Zacchaeus. After the way he had stolen from them by collecting more than he should, he didn't deserve any respect. So, he climbed a tree to catch a glimpse of Jesus.

He must have looked funny—a man dressed in his business robe sitting in a tree! Some must have snickered. But did Jesus? No! He knew what Zacchaeus craved more than anything—some respect, and He gave him what he needed, not what he deserved. "Zacchaeus," He said so all could hear, "I'm going to your house to eat with you today."

The crowd gasped! In that culture the highest honor and esteem anyone could give another was to eat with him in his home. Not one of those along that Jericho street that day would have been caught dead in Zacchaeus' house, let alone found eating with him. And even if they would have, they certainly wouldn't have broadcast their intentions.

What happened when Jesus made that announcement? Zacchaeus' love cup was so filled to overflowing with the undeserved respect Jesus showed him that without a lecture, he immediately said, "I'm going to give back everything I've taken, plus." That's the power of respect!

Respect should not depend upon whether it is deserved. Zacchaeus' situation is not the only time Christ stepped out of the role of what was expected and showed utmost respect to the undeserving. Remember the woman caught in adultery. By law she deserved to be stoned. But Christ ignored the accusations and wrote just enough in the sand for her accusers to see that they weren't blameless. When they left, Christ had a perfect opportunity to give this woman a lecture on purity. Instead, He merely advised her not to do it again.

Later at Simon's feast, Mary poured perfume on Jesus' feet. Simon couldn't understand how Christ, the honored guest, could accept the attentions of a woman whom all recognized as a prostitute. What would it do to His reputation? Obviously, Christ was more interested in the feelings of Mary, than how others felt about Him.

When Simon objected, Jesus had a chance to let it be known just what kind of a scoundrel Simon was. He could have said, "Don't complain, Simon, you were the culprit who seduced Mary. Your sin is worse than hers." However, instead of embarrassing Simon, Jesus told a story. Simon got the message; his dignity was saved.

And then there was Judas. Christ knew he was the betrayer, yet at the Last Supper He placed Judas in an honored position and knelt down to wash his feet. I think I would have let Judas know exactly what I thought of his duplicity. I certainly wouldn't have invited him for supper, let alone wash his dirty feet!

No matter how low they were on the social ladder, no matter how undesirable, no matter how tainted with evil—Christ always treated others with respect. If only we would do the same, what a different world this would be!

A = Acceptance

Loving another person can be a tough job. Especially if he or she isn't pretty, good, or clever. It's a hard but important lesson to learn to accept a person who is different or whose personality clashes with yours. The temptation is to try to remake that person before filling the love cup. Yet, acceptance—the unconditional love of others—is the basis for self-acceptance.

Family advocate Urie Bronfenbrenner once said that every child needs to be loved irrationally. In other words, loved without reason. Loved above and beyond the call of duty. Loved not because you have to give love, but because you choose to give it. Loved for just being.

Irrational love frees people to be themselves. Conditional

love plagues them to continually please the significant people in their lives, on pain of losing their love. Unconditional love accepts with no strings attached. It releases people from the prison of performance.

Think for a moment. How would you feel if you knew your wife wouldn't love you if you didn't get home from work at a specific time? If after 6 p.m. she would ignore you all evening? If after 7:00 she'd throw your supper in the trash? And after 8:00 she'd make you sleep on the couch? How would you feel?

About 5:45 you'd start to panic. Would you make it home on time? Going home would soon become a burden. Instead of the place you really wanted to be, home would be a place you were forced to be, whether you wanted to be there or not. When you did make it on time and your wife was properly loving, you'd feel that she was being nice because you were a "good boy." You wouldn't feel loved just for being you, yourself, but for pleasing her. You would wonder, "What kind of a person am I if I'm not worthy of being loved all the time?" And your feelings of personal value would deteriorate.

She might, indeed, love you all the time, but by her actions you receive a different message. Therefore, you would be forced to act "good" if you wanted her love and attention.

When parents get angry, criticize, or express disappointment, children, likewise, have a difficult time believing they are loved just because they exist. The result is a love hunger that becomes more and more pronounced through the years, wreaking havoc in adult relations. Those who test love, show hostility, are jealous, or don't feel worthy of love and attention are usually individuals who thought they were loved conditionally during childhood.

F = Forgiveness

It was a terrible mistake. I bashed the fender of our brand new car—my husband's dream car—that we had spent a fortune to obtain! On the first day I drove "his" car, I misjudged a block wall. A sickening crunch! There went the fender.

I couldn't believe it. I felt ill. Never in my life had I done such a thing. Why now?

I knew how much the car meant to my husband, Jan; in desperation I began calling for help.

"Body shop? How long will it take you to fix a dented fender on a Mercedes?"

"A week or two."

I pleaded. "But you don't understand, it's got to be fixed by five o'clock tonight."

"Sorry, Lady."

Shop after shop, the same reply.

I knew there was no escaping it. I was going to have to face up to Jan. I tried to think of excuses; some reason, but I drew a blank; I had no excuse. I just misjudged that wall.

Too soon, five o'clock neared. I was nervous. Jan was usually understanding—but I had never before dented his car. I implored the children: "Don't tell Daddy what I did. Let me tell him." But they couldn't restrain themselves. They met Jan on the driveway and yelled, "Daddy, you won't believe what Mommy did!"

"What did she do?"

"Daddy, it's terrible; it's really, really bad."

"Children, what did your mother do?"

"Daddy, it's so bad—that she told us not to tell you that she dented the Mercedes!"

So by the time he gave me my usual hug and kiss, he

already knew about the condition of his car. He wasn't angry. He just shrugged his shoulders and said, "Accidents happen. At least no one was hurt!"

I wanted to get it repaired right away; Jan wasn't too concerned. He said, "There's no rush. You might dent it again and then we could have both dents fixed at the same time!"

We laughed and the incident was forgotten—at least Jan never brought it up again.

Can you imagine how miserable my life would have been if every time I drove Jan's car, he would remind me, "Watch the block walls!" Each reminder of that mistake would have been like reopening a healing wound and rubbing salt in it. Ouch! By choosing not to recall the mistakes of others—or ourselves—healing can occur.

That's the essence of forgiveness—accepting that no one is faultless. We all make mistakes. Why should misjudgment, carelessness, or even spite disrupt a family relationship and empty our love cups? They need not, if the person who errs is forgiven, and the incident is forgotten.

God knows that the road toward reconciliation is paved with the asking for and the granting of forgiveness. He set for us the ultimate example when Jesus forgave those who killed Him. He has also promised: "I'll bury your mistakes as deep as the deepest sea." If God is willing to forgive us, how much more should we be willing to forgive each other?

T = Trust

"Sure I love my husband, but I can't trust him again after what he did," a jilted wife confided. I replied, "If you can't fully trust, you can't fully love."

It's as simple as that. Trust is an inherent part of a loving relationship. It sets the loved one free to be a person, to make decisions, accept consequences, and grow toward his or her personal potential. You should never marry someone you cannot fully trust.

But trust has two dimensions, inextricably linked: *trusting* and *being trustworthy*. You can't trust a person who isn't trustworthy. Nor can you prove you are trustworthy unless someone takes the risk to trust you.

It's foolish to trust someone blindly. You don't hand your wallet to the pickpocket. You don't confide in the town gossip. Neither do wise parents leave the cookie jar within reach of hungry children and expect to have some left for company. Loving trust doesn't mean you must be gullible or a pushover. Encouraging someone to take advantage of you leads to disrespect.

The other extreme is paranoia, or at least chronic skepticism. Being constantly suspicious of everyone is just as debilitating as being an easy mark. Appropriate trust is believing in someone when you have fair evidence of trustworthiness. Sure, there is risk involved in a relationship of trust. The benefits are usually worth the risk.

During the first year or two of a baby's life, parents must demonstrate their trustworthiness. A baby cries, Mom appears to find out what's wrong. A toddler scrapes a knee, Dad applies a Band-Aid and a kiss. Once the lesson that "I can trust my world" is learned, the child is ready to test just how trustworthy it really is! Boundaries are bumped against, and if they remain firm, the child feels secure in a trustworthy world. This is the first and most important prerequisite for good mental health.

Then slowly the tables are turned. To continue growing toward healthy maturity, the child must be trusted to make decisions that are appropriate for his or her age and judgment. How to set the stage for good decision making and then to step back and trust the child is one of the most difficult lessons parents must learn. It's easier—and safer—to just continue making decisions for a child. But love demands trust. Love will not control. Love allows freedom—but freedom within boundaries set by love.

In every aspect of love, God has provided us an example. And so it is with trust. The best example is God Himself; He is completely trustworthy. Every promise He makes, He keeps. Every prophecy has happened exactly as foretold. Read Isaiah 53 and 61—a prophecy foretelling the coming Messiah. Specific details of Christ's life are described, almost as if it were written after the fact. Jesus recognized this prophetic passage and quoted Isaiah 61 as He began His public ministry in Nazareth.

> The Spirit of the LORD GOD is upon Me,
> Because He has anointed Me
> To preach the gospel to the poor.
> He has sent Me to heal the brokenhearted,
> To preach deliverance to the captives . . .
> To set at liberty those who are oppressed,
> To preach the acceptable year of the LORD. . . .
> (See Luke 4:18-19.)

We can trust God. At the gates of Eden He said to Lucifer:

> And I will put enmity
> Between you and the woman,
> And between your seed and her Seed;

> He shall bruise your head,
> And you shall bruise His heel
>> (Genesis 3:15).

Calvary was the fulfillment. An incredible gift of love. But that's not the end. Jesus said, "I go to prepare a place for you. And if I go and prepare a place for you, I will come again and receive you to Myself; that where I am, there you may be also" (John 14:2-3).

Yes, we can trust God. Jesus went back to heaven to prepare a place for us, but He is coming again. God even foretold how "they will see the Son of Man coming on the clouds of heaven with power and great glory. And He will send His angels with a great sound of a trumpet" (Matthew 24:30, 31).

We can be certain that this is true, because God is trustworthy. But the flip side of the coin is that God trusts us. He has already given us the incredible sacrificial gift of His love—the gift of salvation. And even though we are not trustworthy, God loves us so much that He won't manipulate and force us to accept His gift. He leaves the choice to us. That's trust!

CRAFT

Love too often is a nice warm feeling that is as illusive as trying to catch a rainbow. Love, they say, makes the world go round, but if you don't know what that powerful potion really is, you can't harness it and allow it to make a difference in your life.

But define love as *care, respect, acceptance, forgiveness,* and *trust,* and you can begin to understand what it really is. You can choose to *care* for another's needs. That's love. You can choose to treat others with *respect*, even when they may not deserve it. That's love. You can show unconditional *acceptance* and treat a person kindly even if you can't approve of some of his or her behavior. That's love. And you can choose to *forgive*, whether or not the erring one is repentant. Plus, you can choose not to recall hurtful incidents caused by others. Instead, replace those painful memories with something positive. You can, because of the power of love. And talking about power; you have the choice to be trustworthy—keeping the promises you make to yourself and to others. And you have the choice to trust others appropriately so they can experience the incredible freedom of love.

Love is more—much, much more. It will be our study for eternity. But right now, to make it practical, just remember CRAFT. *Care, Respect, Acceptance, Forgiveness,* and *Trust.* When you do, you'll discover how your love will create love in the lives of those you touch. And of all the things in the world, that's probably the most important!

> Love is . . .
> *Care* when you have a personal need.
> *Respect* when shown a kindly deed.
> *Acceptance* regardless of what you do.
> *Forgiveness* that makes all things new.
> *Trust* in others; being trustworthy too.
> Love is...
> something that keeps on giving to you.

Chapter Four

Showing You Really Care

*"It is the time you have wasted for your rose
that makes your rose so important."*
—*Antoine de Saint-Exupery*

Care. The very sound of the word invokes visions of hard, time-consuming work, whether it's care of a house, a lawn, a garden, or the care of a toddler, a patient, or an elderly person. Care in most cases means being tied down, responsible for something or someone who can't survive alone. Care always takes time and many times money: the two most precious and selfishly guarded commodities of our generation. Time and money!

Yet care is the most basic and action-oriented aspect of love. We can't love without caring for the needs of others.

44 · · · ·

How care builds self-worth

It's not good enough to perform an act of caring and at the same time resent it. Without the attitude of love, care can backfire. It can have an adverse effect on self-worth. The way we care can be enhancing or demeaning. Here is how it works.

People feel valuable when they perceive that others accept them as *competent* and *desirable*. Sometimes, being in a state of need diminishes competency to zero. It's true with the newborn—the aged too. Then self-worth is determined by how desirable the person feels. This can be a time of real vulnerability. The person who gives care must make the helpless feel accepted and even desirable. If not, that person's self-worth is likely to suffer.

If the period of helplessness is brief, such as a bout with the flu, and competency returns, then recovery from a period of harsh, unloving care is possible. But if helplessness is long-term—throughout childhood—the damage to the person's self-worth may be irreversible.

Early life is the most helpless time for children, a time when the child's sense of acceptance and desirability is most vulnerable to the type of care received. The way you care will either enhance or diminish a child's self-worth. But it's not easy to provide care with a loving touch when you're tired, frustrated, and close to burnout. It's difficult to fill from an empty cup!

It is also possible for our care to blur children's images of competency and thus mar their sense of self-worth. It is not loving to continue doing something for children after they can benefit by doing it themselves. This tendency to over-protectiveness takes away children's sense of self-worth that could be gained by successfully doing things for themselves.

· · · · **45**

Creating Love

Our concept of self is formed as a result of numerous interactions with the significant people in our lives. If those interactions carry the message that we're competent and desirable, we believe it and grow toward that ideal. If the message is that we're incompetent and worthless, we tend to believe that, irrespective of whether it's true or false.

The self-concept is basically a reflection of how people perceive that others see them. So often it is the way we care that portrays the most vivid picture. If we can care with love and respect, even when people are disagreeable, then they begin to view themselves as desirable. When you feel desirable, you can get on with the business of growing into competency.

Finding time to love

Care takes time. Perhaps that's why so many people resent giving care to others. Once the care is given, it often must be repeated again and again. You're never quite finished! This is especially true with young children, the handicapped, or elderly.

In essence, time spent caring is *never* time wasted. It's an investment in the most important product ever produced: another human being. And it's the quality and spirit of your care that will determine, to a great degree, whether or not the significant people in your life will have healthy love cups—or leaky ones! Listen, share, touch—just be there. Give your most precious gift—the gift of your presence.

Extended family support

When my mother was growing up, the average household had three adults. Mom, dad, grandma, uncle, or a hired hand. There was always someone around when the kids needed help—or when a love cup was empty. But what do our children have today? Many are living with only one adult. The balancing act is almost impossible. When frustrations mount and tempers flare, where does a child run for comfort?

Watch the rhythm of two parents' interactions with a child. One comes home shouting, "I told you to mow the lawn before I got home," and the other gives the child a squeeze and an extra cookie for dessert. When one steps to the authoritarian side of the teeter-totter, the other, without really thinking about it, moves to the nurturing side.

Balance. A single parent is preforming a high-wire act, trying to balance authority and nurturance all at the same time with no safety net of loving adults (spouse, grandparents) to fall back on. What a responsibility it puts on the rest of us to be this safety net for the moms, dads and children living in one-parent homes. We can fill cups by offering to keep the kids so Mom can have a night off, or by inviting them over for hot oatmeal cookies and a glass of cold milk to break the after-school loneliness until Dad gets home from work. Our care for the welfare of children must not end when our own fly the nest. Look around. With half of the kids in the country some time in their lives living with a single adult, the chances are great that there are some empty cups down the block from you needing a little love and attention.

Grandparents are a wonderful source of support, but if your children's real grandparents aren't close, adopt some. There are many older folks with half-empty cups who would love a family. And they can be wonderful cup fillers for your children. We adopted Grampa George when our kids were small. We found him at church. He had no family and lived alone in his camper. He eagerly accepted an invitation for dinner, and our relationship grew. One weekend Jan and I had made a commitment to be out of town and were shocked to find that the big school program was to be at that same time. "That's okay," the kids said, "Grampa George can take us." Now, in our memory book, there's a picture of Grampa George standing beside "his" kids at that major event.

Guidelines for long-distance grandparenting

If you're a grandparent and not lucky enough to live down the block or across town, here's some long-distance, inexpensive ideas of how you can let those kids know that they're loved.

Young children love surprises—especially little surprises from the grandparents. I remember how my three preschoolers used to jump up and down with delight when they discovered a letter from Grandma in our mailbox because they knew there would be three pieces of sugarless gum in the envelope, one for each of them. One day they were hounding me for some gum, and I kept telling them that I didn't have any. "Why don't you have any?" they asked.

"Because," I said in frustration, "gum costs money."

"Well," they said, "then let's call Grandma and have her send us some gum." (As if the long-distance call wouldn't cost any money!)

When I think back to my childhood, I remember my grandma giving me two things. The first was silly drawings: cartoon-like animals that she sketched. I treasured each drawing. The second was her four-leaf clover plant. I remember her letting me pick those four-leaf clovers and press them in the pages of books for good luck! What a treat!

Here are some cup-filling ideas of things you might want to send to your grandkids:

- Check out garage sales for inexpensive books, toys, or puzzles.
- Make inexpensive picture frames for their original paintings.
- Check with pet stores for free pamphlets or inexpensive charts on pet care.
- Visit the local plant nursery for free slips from plants or a free instruction guide on making a small garden.
- Press flowers and use them to decorate bookmarks or stationery.
- Mount butterflies or beetles.
- Send them advertising stamps (like for magazines, etc.) or decorative seals.
- Send them paper planes or inexpensive kites.
- Give them old clothes and shoes for "dress-up."
- Why not make a funny home video of Grandma and Grandpa?
- Collect funny pictures or jokes.
- Send away for the "free" gifts from cereal boxes.
- Each month ask a different state to send your grandchild information about that state. Usually they have a packet available to send on request. Information about these packets can be obtained from writing to the state department located in each capital city.

It's really not difficult to brighten a young child's day

with a little extra love gift. They don't have to be expensive to be meaningful!

Guidelines for grandparents parenting their grandchildren

Grandparents are some of the greatest cup fillers in the world. A large number, because drugs have destroyed a generation, are parenting their grandchildren. Just the time when they're looking forward to getting back into the work force, doing some traveling, or taking it easier, they find themselves with a houseful of kids. Instead of full-cup kids, however, parental conflict, separation, neglect, and punitive care have emptied their cups. And grandparents are having to deal with the consequences of empty, leaky cups they never experienced with their own children. The job is tougher! And just as the healing starts and the cup begins to fill, there is the chance that the child will be swept back into cup-emptying environments by order of the court or by parental guilt. Here are some cup-filling guidelines for grandparents finding themselves parenting the second time around:

1. *Remember, you are the grandparents—not the parents.* Children are the products of their parents, and their value is wrapped up in their parents. Don't destroy their image of their parents.

2. *Do everything possible to help the children maintain respect for their parents.* You don't have to approve of their behavior. You don't have to be gullible and allow them to use you, but you can treat them with dignity.

3. *When things get tough, get help.* The children you are caring for may have special needs because of their fractured pasts. Read parenting books, take parent-education classes,

but that may not be enough. Family counseling may give you the edge you need to hasten the healing and the filling.

4. *Don't be afraid to discipline.* When children come from broken homes, they are desperately in need of security. Knowing where the boundaries are and knowing there is someone strong enough to keep the boundaries will give the children the security they crave.

5. *But remember, you can only discipline as much as you're willing to love.* Your psychologically bruised and battered little ones are going to need a lot of individual attention. They're going to soak it up. And loving, especially the unlovable, takes energy. You're going to need a lot of it.

But along with the hard work, there will be the rewards. And hopefully you'll end up having a special love "affair" with your grandchildren, like my own father did!

> I love to see your flashing eyes
> when first you run to me.
> With secrets cradled in your head,
> you climb upon my knee
> And put your arms around my neck
> and whisper in my ear
> The words that warm an aging heart:
> "I love you, Grampa dear."
>
> You ride upon my horse's foot
> and jiggle up and down,
> Then comb my hair this way and that,
> as if I were a clown.
> I tickle you in ticklish spots,
> and you cry out for more,
> And then I twirl you round and round,

and land you on the floor.
There's something very special, child,
about our love affair.
Some people may not understand,
but Grandma is aware.
So I can play with you all day.
I'll heed your beck and call,
And I'll grow young just watching you,
my precious baby doll.

Showing care for each family member

Children have physical and psychological needs that must be cared for. But so do parents. A caring attitude toward each member of the family helps develop and bond family loyalty. Children should see Mom caring for Dad and Dad caring for Mom. No one should be exempt from showing kindness to others, regardless of age. To demonstrate the principle that even a baby could contribute something to the happiness of other family members, one mother said she put their new baby in his four-year-old sister's bed to warm it. The older child in turn spent some time each day entertaining her little brother.

I like the idea of a buddy system in the family, where each person has a special responsibility to stick up for someone else, making sure that they get their needs met. Our family enjoyed giving each other a "car wash." That's when the unsuspecting person would be "washed" from all sides with compliments and kind deeds. But the best car wash of all was when we gave it to Opa. Jan's father was lonely after the death of his wife, and one day when we had him over, he was especially grouchy. I reminded the children that when someone is unhappy and makes others miserable, it's probably because of an empty love cup. "Let's give Opa a car wash," the kids shouted. So within minutes we moved in for the wash. "Opa, I love you so much," said Kari, as she gave him a hug. "Here's my favorite book for you to look at," said Kevin. And Kim handed Opa his harmonica saying, "Opa, play your harmonica for me, I love to hear you play." And within minutes, Opa's love cup was full. The grouchiness was gone.

Grant proposal deadlines were tough times for our family, with Jan being involved with research at Loma Linda University. Even though he knew months ahead of time that a deadline was coming, still, those last few days often meant working around the clock, grabbing a sandwich at the Patio Pantry, and pushing on. It had been a couple of days since the kids had seen their daddy—and one more day till the deadline. I explained to the children that Daddy couldn't be home because he was an excellent statistician and needed to put extra time into writing an excellent grant proposal. Then the idea struck. "You know what we could do?" I said. "We could help your daddy by making supper for his staff, so they wouldn't have to spend time going down to the cafeteria." And that's what we did.

I could have been upset during those times when Jan wasn't home. I could have complained, "I can't understand why your daddy doesn't start on his grant proposals earlier so he wouldn't have to neglect us like he's doing." But instead, this became an opportunity to model to the kids how we could care for his needs—even though it was impossible for him to be home meeting ours!

Live-in care for a sick or elderly relative

Caring for a sick or elderly relative in your home can be a meaningful experience for the entire family. The key to success is your attitude. If this is something you take great delight in, your children will tend to respond in a similar vein. If you feel used, tied-down, and resentful, it can destroy your family.

Examine your motives. Caring for another person for money, because of guilt, or because you feel sorry for the person, will only provide short-term motivation. But if you extend long-term live-in care because of the joy of service, the benefits to your family of being able to live an unselfish lifestyle, and because of the satisfaction of filling this person's love cup, the chances are good that it will work.

Consider the following before making a long-term commitment:

How does your family feel about this person living with you? There are so many ways a family can benefit from caring for another person in their home. Your children can learn caring skills, respect for the older generation, and how to entertain others. In return, they will have one more person in the family to fill their love cups. But none of these positive things will happen if the children feel this decision was forced on them.

Is there a private area for this person so the person will not interfere with your family's activities? And if the person needs round-the-clock care, is there someone to provide respite care on a regular basis? If the children have to give up a bedroom for this person, or feel they can't run or play boisterously because it would disturb the person, or if they can't watch the TV programs they want to because the person wants to watch something else, or if they can't go anyplace with their folks because one parent always has to stay home, it's never going to work.

How congenial is this person's temperament? If your husband has always resented his mother-in-law, don't fantasize that having her live in your home is going to suddenly change his feelings. If anything, negative feelings will intensify. Is the person impossible to get along with, filled with complaints, and bitter at the world? Think twice about bringing this influence into your home. If it's an empty love cup that is causing this behavior, there may be a chance your loving care can make a difference in this person's life. But don't count on it!

Are you a care-aholic? Some people become so enmeshed in the care of another that they become tied to the task and cannot view their relationship objectively. They cannot step away and allow others to care. This will cause your family members to become resentful and bitter.

You can't allow the care of another person to drain your love cup. You need refilling. You need private time. And you must be able to keep your priorities in their proper order: your children and spouse must come first. If you feel your priorities slipping because of the demanding nature of the care, you must be willing to hire respite care.

Because long-term live-in care will change the dynamics of your family, it is impossible to know until you try it, whether or not it will be good for your family. If possible, try caring for the person on a short-term, trial basis. If at the end of this time your family feels the benefits outweigh the disadvantages, you can make a longer commitment.

If you feel you have no choice, that there is no other place for this person to be cared for and, therefore, you are forced to extend the care, the chances are great that it won't work. But remember, where there is a problem, there is always a solution. There are always options. If you believe this, you'll look for them, and you'll be surprised what you'll find.

Care beyond the family

Service to others is one of the traits of a strong, healthy family. A family that merely receives and never gives becomes like a stagnant pond—or the Dead Sea. Yet care takes time—and often, money. There's precious little of either commodity needed to care for family members, how can there be anything left for others?

Scripture, however, is plain. "When God's children are in need, you be the one to help them out. And get into the habit of inviting guests home for dinner or, if they need lodging, for the night. When others are happy, be happy with them. If they are sad, share their sorrow" (Romans 12:13-15, TLB).

And then in Matthew 25 is the reminder that when the Lord comes in His glory with all His holy angels and the nations will be before Him, He will separate them and say to those on His right hand, "Come, you blessed of My Father, inherit the kingdom prepared for you from the foundation of the world: for I was hungry and you gave Me food; I was thirsty and you gave Me drink; I was a stranger and you took Me in; I was naked and you clothed Me; I was sick and you visited Me; I was in prison and you came to Me." And when the people ask when they did these things, Jesus says, "Inasmuch as you did it to one of the least of these My brethren, you did it to Me" (Matthew 25:31-46).

If you want to grow caring children, you've got to model it. Start by being thoughtful to those around you. Share what you have with others, be helpful to your neighbors by mowing their lawn when they go on vacation, or babysitting their kids without pay. And as your children grow, encourage them to do the same.

Very early, children should be trained to write a Thank-you note when someone gives them something. If a friend is sick, they can send a get-well card. Take them with you to visit the elderly. Children spark up the atmosphere of a retirement center or convalescent home.

There are so many worthwhile community projects, many of which you can participate in with your children. Care is love in action. You can't teach your children the value of care from a textbook. You've got to get involved. As you reach out, you will discover it is more blessed to give than to receive.

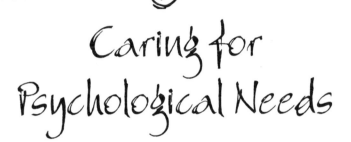

Chapter Five

Caring for Psychological Needs

*"If you really love one another properly,
there must be sacrifice."*
—Mother Teresa

We willingly care for the physical needs of others. These needs jump out at us from the front pages of our newspapers and grab our sympathy and our dollars. The starving children in Somalia need food; those dying of cholera in India need medication and safe drinking water; the displaced of Rwanda need shelter. But what about their emotional needs? Is anyone concerned about their fears, their hopelessness, or their insecurities?

We are trained to care for our children's physical needs. We quickly learn to diaper them, bathe them, to mix the formula or give the breast, and to make sure they get a good night's sleep and an afternoon nap. But children, too, have more than physical needs. They have psychological needs: to belong, to feel secure, to have a sense of value. Here's where parents so often fail.

My husband, Jan, was on a business trip. The house was quiet, the children long in bed. Suddenly, I heard muffled sobs. I made my way to six-year-old Kari's bed. "What's wrong?" I asked.

"I don't have any friends at school," she cried. "Nobody played with me today."

"That really makes you feel sad, doesn't it?" I replied.

"Yes," she nodded, "I just wish Jesus would come right now so I wouldn't have to go to school tomorrow."

"I sometimes feel that way too." I sympathized. "What would you like Jesus to have for you in heaven, when He comes?"

We talked about a pretty white colt named Nikki, and other aspects of a child's view of heaven. After a while we discussed her classmates and talked about some ways for her to become better acquainted with them.

"It just takes three magic words," I told her. "All you have to do to make a friend is to go up to someone who looks more lonely than you, smile, and say the three magic words, 'Hi, I'm Kari.' "

Finally I asked, "Do you think you can go to sleep now?"

"Yes, Mommy," she replied, "but may I sleep in your bed tonight?"

"Sure," I said, "Crawl in on Daddy's side."

About an hour later, I was ready for bed. There, sound asleep on my pillow was Kari. Next to her was a little pink card. I picked up the card and read some scribbly printing;

"Dear Mommy, I love you. Love, Kari."

It was hard to believe. Kari's first letter was a love note to me. What had I done to deserve it? She had called for care; I had comforted her. And my reward was a precious keepsake. Tears welled in my eyes. What a sweet child. I crawled into bed, put my arm around Kari, and slept next to her all night.

What had I done? I cared for her psychological need for comfort by listening to her, and that care so filled her love cup, that it overflowed to fill my own.

Caring for the physical *and psychological* needs of others is a prime component of love: perhaps the most active, surely the most basic.

Family members as psychological supporters

Family members are the most important agents for meeting first-stage psychological needs, so deprivation won't lead to dysfunction. But unfortunately, very little time is given to training individuals to be psychological supporters. So instead of reacting with rational understanding to the emotional needs of our spouses or children, we too often react by the "seat of our pants" and allow our own feelings to temper our responses. In the end, instead of being helpful, we become a part of the problem, making things worse. That's why it's often said: a family member is a counselee's worst counselor.

Although I, too, would question the wisdom of a family member acting as a counselor, there is an essential role that moms, dads, siblings, grandparents, aunts, uncles, and cousins should play, indeed, must play to keep family members psychologically healthy. And that's the role of a psychological supporter.

Caring for Psychological Needs

A psychological supporter prevents emotional problems from developing by meeting each member's basic hierarchy of needs. Take Maslow's hierarchy of needs, for example: The most basic need is *physiological*: for air, food, drink, and rest. The next level has to do with *safety*: for security, stability, and freedom from fear, anxiety, and chaos which is achieved with the help of a structure made up of laws and limits. The third level is that of *belongingness and love*: for affection and intimacy that is provided by family, friends, and a lover. *Esteem* is level four: for self-respect and the respect of others. The final level, which is the loftiest need, is to become a *self-actualized* person that comes from doing what you are best suited for and capable of. It is estimated that only one percent of the population actually achieves this level. But for those who do, it is the family who makes it possible.

How do you meet psychological needs?

When your child tearfully says, "Mommy, I don't have any friends at school," what are you tempted to say? "Of course you have friends. Mary's your friend. And what about Andy and Ted?"

When your teenager shocks you with, "Dad, my boyfriend is really pressuring me to go to bed with him. We love each other. I really don't see why it's so wrong." How do you respond? "Let me tell you why it's wrong. Ever heard of AIDS or genital warts? And you could end up pregnant," etc. etc. etc.

When you've had a bummer of a day, nothing's gone right, and finally when your husband gets home, you complain, "I feel so depressed. It's like I'm living in a fog. I can't understand why I can't shake these awful feelings." How do you want him to react? Do you want him to say, "Well, sweetheart, what did you eat for breakfast this morning? And how much exercise have you gotten? Well, no wonder you're feeling depressed!"

No. No. That's the last thing you want him to do. You want him to take you in his arms and cuddle you a little. Maybe let you cry on his shoulders, wipe away your tears. Then maybe after he listens as you share your feelings— and when you're beginning to feel the sun might break through the gloom, maybe then you'll be willing to listen to the good information he's willing to share.

When you have a psychological need, information is the last thing you want. Yet what do we do to our children? They come to us with their emotions in shreds, they're psychologically hurting, and we have a personal need to fix things. We give them wonderful information. The problem is, information given at the time there is a psychological need is seldom wanted or appreciated, and it's almost never acted upon!

Now look back at those typical responses we give our children. Your child doesn't think she has any friends. What should you do? Let her tell you about her problem while you listen!

And the teen who's talking about premarital sex? Listen to her. How is she feeling? Where is she coming from? An appropriate response might be, "It's really difficult to wait when you love a guy and he's pressuring you, isn't it?" Or you might make the comment, "It's tough to deal with the conflict between what your emotions are telling you to do and what your value system is telling you." Now is not the time for a lecture on morals. If you have laid a good foundation and your teen is not acting out of rebellion, trust your training; trust her to make a decision that will not compromise her sensitive conscience. By your willingness to listen without pressuring her, she can discuss the pros and cons and clarify in her own mind the best course of action.

You may not be a trained psychologist. But most psychological needs don't need therapy. They just need someone who is willing to listen and encourage. They don't need information—at least most of the time they don't. If information is needed, kids will ask for it. Then as a courtesy, instead of reciting the textbook or the lecture you composed in your head, which will cause them to never ask you again, you might clarify, "Would you really like to know what I think is best?" and then keep your answer down to 100 words or less!

Lessons in listening from psychologists

Lesson #1: Observe body language. You can tell a lot about the psychological condition of a person by reading body language. Some estimate that 65 percent or more of what is communicated is not through words or tone of voice, but through body language. Does your child, spouse, or friend look scared, unhappy, depressed, angry, confused, frustrated, bitter, or hurt? Take time to make some careful observations and you'll find your response more appropriate and, therefore, more helpful.

Lesson #2: Listen for the tone of voice. Apart from the words said, what do you hear in the voice? If you couldn't understand the language, what emotions would this voice be expressing?

- A high, loud, staccato voice says, "I'm angry!"
- A soft, hesitant voice says, "I'm hurt!"

- A harsh, monotone voice might mean, "I'm bitter!"
- A halting, uncertain voice might mean, "I'm confused!"

Lesson #3: Listen carefully to the message behind the words. A teen may say, "I hate algebra," and mean, "I'm afraid I'm going to flunk the algebra test."

A child might yell, "Why can't you pick me up on time!" and mean, "I'm embarrassed when I don't get to Little League on time."

A husband might comment, "I think I'll just quit my job!" and be asking for words that will bolster his sagging self-worth that tell him he has skills and abilities that are important to you.

Lesson #4: Keep your mouth shut. When you're tempted to add your two cents' worth, don't! It will probably be worth even less! Allow your loved one to talk. Don't interrupt. Even silence can be productive, if it gives the person time to formulate an answer or communicate an important bit of information that might solve the problem.

Lesson #5: Defuse the emotion. Forget the words and focus on the emotion expressed. A good "you feel" statement usually helps. "You feel angry when . . ." If you're not exactly sure of what the person is feeling, a more general response might be, "It's scary when . . ." If you've hit the right emotion and do it without judgment, you'll get a confirmation. Your acknowledgment of a troublesome emotion will give the child permission to talk about it. And when an emotion is talked about and defused, it doesn't have to be acted out. (We'll deal more in depth with this in Chapter 8.)

Lesson #6: Use persuasive, not pushy openings when you'd

like to offer information. Check out the difference.

A persuasive statement might be the following:

- Have you ever considered . . .
- When that happened to me, I . . .
- There are a number of things you could do, such as . . .
- I once read of someone in a similar situation, and he . . .

A pushy statement would be:

- If it were me, I'd . . .
- Why don't you just . . .
- Common sense should tell you . . .
- As far as I can see, there's only one answer . . .

Lesson #7: Point out reality. Some people have a hard time accepting the fact that they are responsible for their own behavior. When they begin the blaming game, or spout off crazy ideas that are totally out to lunch, a good counselor calls their bluff.

When someone begins playing the blame game, a counselor might say something like, "You own your emotions. No one made you do it. The choice was yours. You are responsible for your own behavior. Because of your choice, you are having to suffer this consequence."

Lesson #8: Focus on solutions. Merely spilling emotions may not automatically result in a solution. Sometimes it happens: your child's emotions are defused, thinking clears, and decisions are made. But other times a child may have to be led through the decision-making process.

Step 1: Clarify the problem.
Step 2: Brainstorm solutions.
Step 3: Evaluate ideas.
Step 4: Select the best.
Step 5: Decide when the solution will be implemented.
Step 6: After implementation, evaluate it's success.

Lesson #9: Encourage positive self-talk. A good counselor inspires self-confidence in the counselee. A support person may not always be around to fill empty love cups. That's why you must encourage individuals to be strong, to make decisions, and to take responsibility for their own lives. You're not going to always be around to inspire confidence, so it's important you help them gain self-confidence by trashing their negative self-talk and replacing it with positive talk.

When someone says something negative like, "I'm no good at that," listen to the emotion behind the statement, point out reality, and then encourage the positive. For example: "I may not be the best tennis player in the world, but there are many things I can do well." At this point being as specific as possible will be of greatest value.

Lesson #10: Affirm personal value. Personal value is not determined by money, age, status, rank, friends, or looks. Show you value others just because they exist. Treat each one with respect, regardless of what the person has done. Hold your anger and criticism—and encourage, encourage, encourage.

Care giving versus enabling

Sensitive, caring people who find it easy to empathize with the psychological needs of others can, without thinking, become a part of the problem rather than the solution by trying to fix things.

Psychological strength and feelings of personal value are achieved by taking control of one's own life. This includes finding solutions to personal problems. If one family member takes on too much responsibility for fixing someone else's problem, that person ceases to be a care giver and becomes an enabler, robbing the other person of the satisfaction of making personal choices. This only makes the problem worse. Now, not only does the person have the problem, but adding insult to injury, the person now feels controlled by the enabler. The result? More emotional baggage is stacked on the previous load. The whole family suffers.

My mom was an enabler. My brother hit hard times and needed money. But she loved him and wanted to help, so she gave him the money. But in the giving, she felt she had a right to openly criticize his financial decisions. The problem was, she never allowed him to suffer from those decisions and thus learn more responsible behavior. Instead, she doled out more. But more was never enough. And her critical attitude was like a noose around his neck. She felt used. He felt controlled. Twenty-five years of hindsight have opened the eyes of the whole family, including my brother's, as to the tragedy of a mom usurping the rightful responsibility of a child to make his own decisions and suffer the consequences—good or bad—that may have resulted.

Enabling is not really love! It may seem like the loving thing to do to try to smooth the road for a stumbling child, husband, wife, or parent. But if it steals the decision-making responsibility from that person, it also steals the sense of competence, satisfaction, and self-worth that person would have gained by finding his or her own solution. In the end the person has not learned a better way. For it is the consequences suffered that provide the motivation for change.

Caring for the psychological needs of another means to listen, to encourage, to comfort, and to lovingly confront. This caring support is like a springboard, giving others an extra boost of strength and courage to make the decisions they need to make. Regardless of the consequences, the spring board—the support system—will always be there. Don't make the jump for another; don't take the decision-making responsibility away; don't control; don't enable the person to continue in a self-destructive course. Instead, a healthy family will be there to care, to respect, to accept, to forgive, and to trust, to continue to be a springboard for launching. That's what we all need from others.

The use of touch in meeting psychological needs

One of my graduate students, who was also a nurse, told me about an unnerving experience. As she began to put a blood-pressure cuff on an elderly woman's arm, the woman began to weep. The nurse was alarmed. Her voice mirrored concern. "Am I hurting you?" she asked. "No," sobbed the woman, "It's just that no one has touched me since my husband died four years ago."

Touch is important at every age. It symbolizes desirability; people avoid repulsive things. A baby requires a lot of touching in order to develop normally. In fact, touching promotes physical as well as psychological well-being. But what about older children and adults? Here's a smattering of the research:

- Kids who are hugged, especially by their dads, have healthier feelings about their bodies than others (Sandra Weiss, University of California School of Nursing in San Francisco).

- College students who were touched on their arms during a regular teacher conference had a higher admiration for their teachers, and they scored a significant six points higher on their next exam than "untouched" classmates (Memphis State University.)

- In a thirty-six-year study that began when the subjects were kindergartners, parental warmth was shown to produce preteens with greater self-esteem and young adults capable of more congenial relationships. At age forty-one, those who had been raised with the most affection were most likely to have long and relatively happy marriages, raise children, develop close friendships, pursue outside interests, and to feel generally happier and less stressed (Carol E. Franz, Boston University).

- Patients who receive gentle therapeutic touching experience a drop in blood pressure and an increase in oxygen-carrying hemoglobin in their blood. After a thirty-minute massage there is a drop in the body's levels of cortisone and adrenaline, which are indicators of excess stress (Dolores Krieger, New York University).

- Adults who live alone die sooner from every kind of disease than do those who are married. One reason postulated is that isolated people simply don't get touched enough. Touching triggers physiological and biochemical changes known to help protect the body against heart disease, cancer, infection, and stress-related illness (James Lynch, University of Maryland).

Creating Love

It's all pretty convincing, isn't it! Yet as children grow older and no longer need a lot of physical care, touching them is less automatic. I'm concerned that many older children and teenagers aren't receiving the touching they need to keep their love cups full.

Studies of teenage pregnancies confirm this suspicion. These girls often report that they received little or no touching from their fathers. Maybe they did as little kids, being bounced on Daddy's knee, thrown in the air, and landing safely in his strong arms, being carried off to bed or getting their tummies tickled with his rough whiskers. But then, something changed. Sometime around eight or ten years of age, the hugging and playing stopped. Not all at once; it tapered off. This left a void in their lives. They needed to be close to someone. They wanted to be hugged. With awakening sexuality, these needs loomed ever larger. They weren't met within the family; in time, the girls turned elsewhere. The result: a pregnancy, almost always unwanted.

Touch is one of the most misunderstood and under-used treasures of love available to families and friends. It is there to communicate care, respect, acceptance, forgiveness, and trust. In fact, it is a far more dynamic way of saying "I love you" than words alone.

But because touch is the most effective way to say "I love you," it is equally as volatile when used inappropriately.

- A loving touch says you're desirable. A harsh one destroys personal value.
- A loving touch bonds. A harsh one destroys.
- A loving touch smooths conflicts and hastens reconciliation. A harsh one is a precursor to alienation.

- A loving touch comforts. A harsh one causes pain.
- A loving touch promotes security. A harsh one increases fear, uncertainty, and self-doubt.

It's the inappropriate touch that blisters and bruises, leaving a child's body aching in pain. And it's the warped touch that fondles private places and violates a child's innocence, sexually abusing. The result: cups so shattered and broken that a lifetime of therapy merely patches, leaving the pieces for God to put together with His supreme love—the glue that can make all things new.

Touch as a psychological healer

The lowest quality interaction that people may have is to simply think about one another and to communicate the fact that they are thinking about each other. I often say that's worth one point. The love note, the telephone call. They're important but not nearly as important as being together. Being together is worth two points! Once you're together, you can begin adding more quality to your relationship by talking together. That's worth three points. When you really focus on each other and look into each other's eyes, that's a four-pointer. And for five points? You guessed it. Touch!

Healing a relationship works in the very same way. If you have wronged someone and want reconciliation, the quickest and most meaningful way is to reach out and touch the other person. (It's worth five points.) Next, say "I'm sorry," face-to-face, but without a touch. (That's a four-pointer.) Third, just saying the words will work, but it's only worth three points. Choosing to be close to the person you've wronged and never bringing up the misunderstanding and talking about it could be counted as two points. Although not as meaningful, it is better than remaining apart and merely thinking that you should say, "I'm sorry," which is only worth one point! Yes, there is something magically mending in a touch. It can make a reconciliation a five-point experience.

After a seminar about the importance of touch in the lives of our teenagers, a mother came up to me with tears in her eyes saying, "What you have said about the healing power of touch is so true." This was her story. Her teenage son had grown rebellious. He refused to listen to his folks, and they could no longer control where he went or when he came home. One night after they had gone to bed, he rushed through the house and into their bedroom screaming, "I'm on a bad trip. Help me! Don't leave me alone. Let me sleep with you!"

Dad called a physician friend and received the advice: "Keep an eye on him until it wears off." So Dad and Mom scooted over in their king-sized bed and put this hunk of a seventeen-year-old between them. All night they listened to his breathing, felt his forehead, and kept in almost constant contact with him. The next morning when the boy awoke, he couldn't believe, that they loved him enough to share their bed with him after the way that he had treated them. That was the beginning of his homecoming. And he said it was the sense of his folks's presence and touch throughout the night that got the love message across.

Jesus' ministry is an incredible example of the importance that touch played in the healing process. Just follow Jesus through the Gospel of Luke and notice how He healed:

Luke 4:40: After Jesus healed Peter's mother-in-law all the sick were brought to Him, and it says, "He laid His hands on every one of them and healed them."

Luke 5:13: A leper came and asked for healing and Jesus "put out His hand and touched him, saying, 'I am willing; be cleansed.'"

Luke 6:17-19: In this passage it speaks of a great multitude of people from all Judea and Jerusalem and from the seacoast of Tyre and Sidon that came to be healed of their diseases. "And the whole multitude sought to touch Him, for power went out from Him and healed them all."

Luke 7:12-14: The widow's son was raised from the dead. "Then He came and touched the open coffin, and those who carried him stood still. And He said, 'Young man, I say to you, arise.'"

Luke 8:43, 44: The woman with the flow of blood "came from behind and touched the border of His garment. And immediately her flow of blood stopped."

Luke 8:54: Jairus's daughter was raised from the dead. "But He put them all out, took her by the hand and called, saying, 'Little girl, arise.'"

Luke 13:13: A woman had an infirmity for eighteen years and couldn't stand up straight. "And He laid His hands on her, and immediately she was made straight, and glorified God."

Jesus' ministry is an example of how we should minister. He first cared for the people's needs, which in most cases involved the accepting gesture of touch, and then he spoke of spiritual matters. Why didn't He do it the other way around? Perhaps because ministries involve people who desperately need their lives and/or their pain to be significant. They need their situation to be real, to matter to someone other than themselves. *Real* is precisely what people become to one another at the intersections of life—when they touch."

Jesus became real through touch, and you can too. When

the people you care for feel your touch, when you validate their personhood through touch, you become real to them. At that intersection of life, they will be far more open to information, including spiritual matters.

To care is to become real

Servant care—meeting another's needs without expectations of getting something in return—has its own reward. As you give of yourself in a close, meaningful relationship that involves time and touch, you will experience attachment. A link to another human being. A connection.

The psychological energy generated from the sense of belonging that grows out of a caring relationship is worth every minute of time you were willing to invest.

Margery Williams, in the classic children's storybook, *The Velveteen Rabbit*, sums up the value of care in these often-quoted words that the Skin Horse said to the Velveteen Rabbit when the Velveteen Rabbit asked, "What is REAL?"

Real isn't how you are made . . . It's a thing that happens to you. When a child loves you for a long, long time, not just to play with, but REALLY loves you, then you become real. It doesn't happen all at once . . . you become. It takes a long time. That's why it doesn't often happen to people who break easily, or have sharp edges, or who have to be carefully kept. Generally, by the time you are REAL most of your hair has been loved off, and your eyes drop out and you get loose in the joints and very shabby. But these things don't matter at all, because once you are REAL you can't be ugly, except to people who don't understand.

Chapter Six

Respecting One Another

"All true love is grounded on esteem."
—George Villiers Buckingham

"*re spect* (ri spekt') n. [L. *respectus*] 1. a feeling of high regard, honor, or esteem [to have *respect* for a great artist] 2. a state of being held in honor or esteem [to have *respect* for one's sons] 3. deference or dutiful regard [*respect* for the law] 4. consideration; courteous regard [to have respect for the feelings of others] —SYN. see REGARD (*Webster's New World Dictionary*).

I wonder how different this world would be if everyone lived out this dictionary definition of respect within their families, among their friends, and when associating with colleagues and strangers. Respect is an important part of

Creating Love

love, treating others with high regard, honor, and esteem.

But unfortunately, too often the real world is the opposite: hostile, cold, and uncaring. Humans have an unfortunate way of treating with disrespect those who are weak or unlike themselves. Think about it. Adults do it to children, children to adults. Whites do it to Blacks, Blacks to Whites. The rich to the poor, the poor to the rich. Protestants to Catholics, Catholics to Protestants, and children to other children, especially those who are different. No matter what size, shape, intelligence, or color, lack of respect for others is a widespread problem. It's a basic reason why so many people have half-filled or empty love cups.

Respect and human nature

Respect implies consideration for the right of another to be unique and free to make age-appropriate decisions. Force and manipulation have no part in a respectful relationship.

It is a truism that you will find in every person what you seek. If you see people as sinful, you will find sin. But if you see them as God's creation, you will find their potential for good.

Let's respect children as members of God's creation. Each has individual needs, different abilities, and a growing capacity to reason and accept consequences. Let's treat children with the dignity they deserve. Let's be courteous and kind as well as firm and consistent. Let's look for the good in the child rather than dwelling on the bad. God's salvation makes it possible for us to do this; Christ's example shows us how.

Take yourself back to that Judean hillside where Jesus is surrounded by people clamoring for His attention and help. The disciples are trying to bring those with special needs to the attention of their Master.

Off to the side you see a group of women move toward Jesus—mothers and grandmothers—with little ones in their arms and children hanging on to their skirts. They desire the Messiah's blessing to be given to their children, but they realize that the only way to get through the pressing crowd is to ask the Master's disciples for help. Surely they will open a way for them.

And then disappointment. Jesus' disciples shake their heads and attempt to shoo the children away. Jesus has far weightier matters to attend to, the men explain, than merely blessing children. There are the sick, the demon-possessed, the crippled, the blind. Realizing the hopelessness of the situation, the women turn to go.

But wait. Jesus hears the children's squeals of laughter and notices what is happening. Calling to His disciples He says, "Let the children alone, don't prevent them from coming to me." And then He makes a lesson out of it for those who so often push children around or push them away. "God's kingdom is made up of people like these" (Matthew 19:14, *The Message*).

Another day, another lesson. This time the disciples have been arguing over who is the highest ranked in God's kingdom.

For an answer Jesus called over a child, whom he stood in the middle of the room, and said, "I'm telling you, once and for all, that unless you return to square one and start over like children, you're not even going to get a look at the kingdom, let alone get in. Whoever becomes simple and elemental again, like this child, will rank high in God's kingdom.

· · · · **77**

What's more, when you receive the childlike on my account, it's the same as receiving me.

"But if you give them a hard time, bullying or taking advantage of their simple trust, you'll soon wish you hadn't. You'd be better off dropped in the middle of the lake with a millstone around your neck. Doom to the world for giving the God-believing children a hard time! Hard times are inevitable, but you don't have to make it worse—and it's doomsday to you if you do (Matthew 18: 1-7, *The Message*).

How often have we given our children, or those we live with, a hard time, bullying or taking advantage of them? "It's doomsday for you if you do," is pretty strong language! Let this be fair warning to many who resort to using their size, power, or position to get their children or weaker individuals to do their bidding!

Treating your child as your best friend

Would you grab your best friend by the arm and drag her through a store? Would you interrupt a friend in the middle of a job when you could wait until he was finished? Would you yell at a friend, "Quit bugging me!" when he needed your help? Would you embarrass a friend in front of others by saying her hair looked like a mop? Would you threaten a friend if he didn't drink his milk or clean up a spill? Would you bribe a friend to brush his teeth? Would you read a friend's mail without asking? Of course not, yet we often treat our children in these ways.

I once read an Erma Bombeck column were she said she thought she always treated her children as she did her best friends until she pretended that two good friends came to dinner and she said things to them that she had at times said to her children. It went something like this:

"Well, it's about time you got here. Where have you been? Leave those shoes outside, John. They're all muddy. And shut the door. Were you born in a barn?"

Or, "John, stop snacking, or you'll ruin your dinner. I didn't work over a hot stove all day to have you nibbling yourself too full to eat!"

And imagine saying something like this to your guests, "What's the matter, John? You're fidgeting. Of course, you have to go to the bathroom. It's down the hall, first door on the left. And don't leave a towel in the middle of the floor when you're finished."

How about these comments?

"Did you wash your face before you came, Joan? Is that a dark spot around your mouth? Don't tell me your hands are clean—I saw you playing with the dog! Joan, don't talk with your mouth full. No one can understand a word you're saying."

Erma Bombeck ended her column by saying that when her son walked into the room, she decided to treat him like a guest. "How nice of you to come," she said pleasantly.

He got nervous. "Now what did I do?" he asked!

I was at a woman's retreat where a gripping testimony was given by a woman about the sexual abuse she had suffered at the hands of a neighborhood gang. There wasn't a dry eye in the room. A few hours later as a part of my presentation, I read Erma Bombeck's column and everyone laughed. We could all see ourselves saying these things to our children, and yet, how absurd to think of saying them to guests!

Creating Love

After my presentation a woman came up to me and said, "Everyone wept when the woman told about the sexual abuse she suffered, and yet they laughed about saying the things Erma Bombeck mentioned. But I cried. You see, my folks constantly said those things to me. And with each barb they tore away a piece of my self-concept, killing me little by little. I feel the psychological abuse I suffered from my parents' constantly putting me down was just as destructive as sexual abuse!"

It's never too early to begin treating children with respect. Start when they are first born. How often has a tiny baby resisted giving up a favorite toy or wiggled while being diapered? All babies do; to fight with them is futile: it only makes them resist even more. Respect their feelings and you'll find them more willing to cooperate. Courteous treatment defuses a child's resistance. Treat a child with respect and you'll have a better chance of getting the same in return.

Earning respect

Ideally, respect need not be earned. Realistically, it must. Too many parents demand respect while acting in ways that tend to make children rebel. How does your child conform to your wishes—out of fear, or out of love and respect?

Would you respect your boss if he jumped up and down threatening, "I'll fire you if you don't do as I say." Of course not. You might fear him and out of fear, follow his instructions, but your respect for him would be nil.

People who are impatient and lose control of their emotions risk emptying love cups and losing respect.

One of the most tragic family breakups I ever observed began with the husband criticizing and demeaning his wife in front of their family and friends. Within months, the children followed suit, hurling hurtful words at their mother. The disrespect grew; her authority was challenged at every move. Life became chaotic. After a divorce, it took months, even years, for her to regain the respect of her children. But imperfectly. At times, her children still resorted to disrespectful behavior. Bad habits are hard to break.

Passing the love test

There are times in a relationship when treating a person with respect is extremely difficult because of his or her abrasive actions. Yet if you can understand the psychological dynamics causing these actions, it is easier to look beyond that behavior to the individual and meet that person's needs rather than merely reacting to their behavior.

Medical personnel must do this daily. Patients who are hurting, irritable, and medicated with mood-altering drugs may complain, blame, demand, and threaten. But the nurse or aide doesn't get angry and treat them disrespectfully. It's the situation that is causing this obnoxious behavior; it's not a personal vendetta.

Strange, it's a lot easier being objective about a stranger's irritating behavior than it is toward someone you live with. Family members need training to see the reason behind certain obnoxious behaviors and how through cup filling, rather than cup emptying, the person's needs can be met. One such situation is when a loved one gives you a love test. Passing it doesn't happen by chance. It takes training to perceive when you're being tested, and coaching to know how to pass! Children are experts at love testing, especially when they think a baby might be loved more than they are. The test usually consists of the worst behavior they can think of. Parents fail if they react with anger and punishment. They win if they begin filling the empty love cup. This doesn't mean you condone the behavior, but correction is much better accepted on a full cup than an empty one!

Children aren't the only ones who love test—husbands and wives at times may test just to see how much they are loved. In fact, if you're a working mom and have a husband who doesn't lift his hand to help around the house, the problem might be that you're flunking your husband's love tests.

Let me explain by describing a typical situation where hubby may be love testing.

Dad arrives home from work first and dismisses the baby sitter who leaves three starving youngsters behind. Dad, knowing Mom will be home shortly, ignores their whining and goes over to the TV and turns on the evening news loud enough to drown out the kids.

Minutes later, Mom opens the door and discovers chaos. The house looks like a national disaster zone, toys are strewn all over the floor, and the kids are fighting and screaming, "I'm hungry." And in the midst of it all lies hubby, nonchalantly watching TV.

How can a man be so oblivious to what's going on around him?

Mom's immediate reaction is to yell, "Can't you ever help around here? This place is a mess and the children are starving. At least you could have gotten them something to eat!" Sound familiar? Well, it may sound familiar, but this type of criticism seldom works!

Actually, there may be a number of reasons why hubby doesn't help around the house. His father may have been a poor role model and he grew up thinking cleaning and cooking were women's work. Or he may just not see what needs to be done at home—some men don't. And if either of these things are the reason for your husband's behavior, it may take a miracle to turn him around.

But there's one more thing that could be causing this behavior, and if so, you can change your man overnight! Do you want to know what it is?

Your husband may feel jealous. He may feel that you love your job or the kids more than you love him. And not liking that conclusion, he unconsciously decides to test you out by doing nothing to help you around the house. This is the love test. If you rant and rave and let him have it verbally, you will flunk his test and he will come to the conclusion that you love the job or the kids more than you love him. If this is the message that your behavior gives him, he will continue testing.

But if you can pass his test and prove to him that you love him supremely, more than the kids and more than the job, he will have no reason to continue testing you.

How can you pass his love test? Well, the next time you walk into chaos, ignore it and go over and give him a big hug and kiss and tell him how much you missed him all day, and how important and wonderful he is and . . . . Yes, he's liable to faint! He knows he doesn't deserve this attention. And he knows what he does deserve!

Your loving behavior, in spite of his obnoxious ways, will prove to him that you do indeed love him. Many times your positive attention will be enough to get your man to ask, "Honey, what can I do to help you out?" And when that happens you'll know that you've passed the love test.

Keeping within psychological boundaries

November 1, 1992, was a picture-postcard day. The bright rays of sun set the hillsides ablaze in riotous shades of gold,

Creating Love

orange, and crimson. Added to the pleasure of beauty was the pleasure of family! My mom, who lived in California, was visiting our Cleveland, Tennessee, home for the first time. What more could I ask?

Now the heavy weekend responsibilities were over and Mom and I were anticipating a fun-filled evening celebrating her youngest grandson, Brett's, fifteenth birthday. We turned right out of our drive and headed south down our little country road toward Calhoun, Georgia, where my sister Dianne and her family lived.

I maneuvered the windy road topping the first hill, then accelerated to forty or forty-five on the straight stretch. Then at the peak of the next hill, life as I had known it came to a shattering halt. A van had strayed across the line and was coming toward me in my lane. I remember the horror of the moment, the screeching brakes, and the immediate impact—and then the deathly stillness pierced only by the stuck horn. After I separated my chest from the steering wheel, I cried, "Mom, Mom, speak to me!" Nothing!

Twenty-two days later my mom died, and I was in a wheelchair. My foot had been severely dislocated—knocked off the leg bone—an injury serious enough that the physicians had at first said there was an 80 percent chance that I'd lose my foot! I walk now and count each step a miracle.

All this heartache, pain, and loss just because someone crossed the line! We buried Mom in Colorado next to my dad, who had died 14 years to the day earlier, and then traveled to California to take care of some of her affairs. All the time I questioned: What lesson can I learn from this awful accident? And then it came to me as I sat in my mom's home church in Calimesa and listened to the words of a song made popular by country singer Ricky Van Shelton,

Keep It Between the Lines. It's about a teenager sitting in the driver's seat of the car with his dad beside him, both very nervous. The teen asks his dad if he really thinks he is ready to drive. Now listen to the words of instruction and encouragement this father gives his son:

> "I'm right here beside you, and you're gonna do fine,
> All you got to do is keep it between the lines.
> 'Cause it's a long narrow road, only the good Lord knows,
> Where it leads in the end, But you've got to begin.
> So keep your hands on the wheel,
> Believe in the things that are real;
> Take your time,
> And keep it between the lines."
> (©1991 careers—BMG Music Publishing, INC. (BMI)—All rights reserved. Used by permission.)

Life is a long, narrow road filled with dangers and disappointments. We don't know the end, but we've got to keep going. Our job is to not give up or lose control and to not hurt others with our emotional pain but to keep our hands on the wheel of our lives, believing in God (for that is real), and taking our time, waiting patiently on the Lord. In short, we must "keep it between the lines."

For just as there are boundaries on highways, lines that cannot be crossed without suffering and death, so there are boundaries in relationships—lines that cannot be crossed without psychological pain and the loss of family and friends. And it's the respect we have for others that will keep us from crossing these lines.

When that young mother looked back to check on her daughter in the back seat and their van crossed the line into my lane, it took away my power of choice. I didn't choose to lie on that cold pavement watching my mom fight for every breath and cry out in pain. I didn't choose to be carried away on a stretcher and suffer the agony of hearing I might be permanently disabled and that my mom probably wouldn't live. My mom didn't choose pain, suffering, and death. It was forced upon us—when someone crossed the line.

Crossing psychological boundaries can cause permanent disability just as much as crossing a physical boundary. And the word we use for "crossing the line" in relationships is abuse. *Abuse is anything that takes away the freedom of choice from another. Anything that forces, manipulates, or controls another person.* Abuse is basically the result of someone crossing the line and imposing his or her will upon another.

We, as Christians, spend a lot of energy fighting things that threaten to control our minds and bodies, such as alcohol, drugs, or hypnotism. If only we would take the same offensive position to stopping the abuse—the inappropriate control, force, or manipulation—that is going on in our homes.

If you truly respect others you won't:

- Use a wooden spoon or a switch on a child every time he strays from the straight and narrow.
- Try to control your husband's behavior with pouting, ridicule, and sarcasm.
- Demand sex or withhold it to punish a spouse.
- Move in with your folks, refuse to look for a job,

shirk house- or yardwork, or threaten them if they won't give you money.

- Threaten divorce or suicide if your husband doesn't toe the line and come home on time.
- Blackmail a sibling, saying, "I'm going to tell, if . . ."
- Deny your wife friends of her own, or deny her the opportunity to get an advanced degree or a job.
- Demean your wife by saying she's stupid and can't do anything right.
- Keep bringing up your husband's mistakes.
- Pout or refuse to talk when someone makes you angry or hurts your feelings.
- Demand an accounting of every cent spent by your husband and check the odometer making sure he can account for every mile.
- Use a child or weaker individual to satisfy sexual desire or as the object of your anger and frustration.
- Blame your parents for your problems.
- Play on the sympathy of your grown children, saying things like "I'll die if you leave me with a stranger or send me to a nursing home."

In other words, out of respect, you will not condone any behavior which crosses the psychological line and imposes one person's will on another.

How can you make sure your behavior is kept between the lines so it won't become abusive? How can you make sure the behavior of others won't be abusive to you?

First, don't allow what others say or do to control you or destroy your sense of value. Keep control of your own emotions, remembering who you really are—a child of God, a royal descendant! Then choose carefully your response. Sometimes this may mean separating yourself from the abuser or standing up for your personal rights and refusing to enable the abuser to continue this destructive behavior. And other times it may mean choosing to respond with love and respect rather than impulsively reacting when others are angry, critical, or in some other way attempting to control you.

Jesus never allowed others to control His power of choice, even at an early age. Remember the words of His mother when she and Joseph finally found him talking to the scholars at the temple after he had been missing for three days. I can just hear her raising her voice and exclaiming in anger and frustration, "Son, why have you done this to us? Look, your father and I have sought you anxiously" (Luke 2:48, *The Message*).

Any typical twelve-year-old would be highly embarrassed if his mother said something like that to him in public, especially in front of people who were quite taken by his "adult" behavior. A typical response might be: "Don't blame me. You're the one who went off and left me here." But not Jesus. Instead of allowing his mother's criticism to make him feel guilty or angry in return, I can hear Him saying something like this, "Mom, from the time I was a little boy you've been telling me who I really am." And then the words from Luke 2:49: "Why is it that you sought Me? Did you not know that I must be about My Father's business?" Without getting angry, without criticizing her, He allowed his mother to own her emotions, while He took charge of His own. That's respect!

Many of Jesus' teachings centered on encouraging people

to take control of themselves, not allowing others to control their reactions and thus treat them disrespectfully. For example, why did Jesus say such things as:

- "But whoever slaps you on your right cheek, turn the other to him also."
- "If anyone wants to sue you and take away your tunic, let him have your cloak also."
- "And whoever compels you to go one mile, go with him two."
- "Love your enemies."
- "Do good to those who hate you."
- "Pray for those who spitefully use you and persecute you" (Matthew 5:38-44).

These instructions defy the natural impulse. If someone hits you, your immediate response is to hit back, but that would be allowing another person's behavior to control yours. Instead, you are to take control and choose a loving reaction. The Jews had no choice when a Roman citizen asked them to carry their burden for a mile. The natural impulse would be to resent having to do this, but Jesus in essence said, "Tell the person you will carry it for two miles. It's now *your* choice, not theirs. *You* are in control."

God wants to help us be in control of our emotional lives and not let others control us. We must learn how to set boundaries so we can make a conscious decision about how to act respectfully toward someone, rather than reacting impulsively. If you are having trouble in this area, seek professional counseling to learn how to set boundaries so you can become everything God meant you to be.

The second way you can keep from crossing the line and

abusing others is to allow others the freedom to make their own decisions and take the responsibility for the decisions they make. Especially, you must watch your anger, criticism, and pouting. These are strong controlling mechanisms that can easily destroy others, and they definitely fall outside the lines of healthy interactions. Instead, live by the Golden Rule, treating others as you would like to be treated: with care, respect, acceptance, forgiveness, and trust.

Life is a long narrow road, where crossing the lines can be dangerous and deadly. Don't destroy the people you care about by overstepping healthy emotional boundaries and using anger, criticism, withdrawal, force, or manipulation to control others. *Keep it between the lines!*

Chapter Seven

The Power of Unconditional Love

The greatest happiness of life
is the conviction that we are loved,
loved for ourselves, or rather,
loved in spite of ourselves."
—*Victor Hugo*

Unconditional love is the crown jewel of CRAFT. Acceptance regardless of the person's behavior, looks, personality, or attitude. Love for no reason at all, other than that the person exists. It's opening your arms to your runaway who through a life of rebellion brought you nothing but sleepless nights, embarrassment, and heartache. It's *not* saying, "I told you so," when your warning was unheeded. It's Ted Bundy's mother calling him the night he was going to be executed for his hideous crimes of torture and brutal murder and saying, "I love you. You'll always be my son." It's Jesus coming to this world to die for people who nailed Him to the cross. It's irrational! It's superhuman!

But unless acceptance, unconditional love, irrational love, or whatever you might call it, is present in a relationship there will be elements of control or manipulation that cause dysfunction and empty love cups.

Conditional acceptance is a powerfully manipulative tool. Some people crave acceptance; they will do virtually anything for it, even accept physical pain and psychological abuse.

A secretary, married for twelve years, related that at seventeen she had become the wife of a wealthy man she didn't really like. He had some objectionable traits. But she felt sure that her charm and wit would change him for the better.

From a poor family, she craved pretty things, fine food, the "better things" of life, and security. They became hers on their wedding day. But her husband remained aloof. He took her to parties to show her off, only to leave her on the sidelines while he engaged in conversation with his associates. If she left his side without permission, however, the sky came crashing down on her.

He told her what to wear and how to eat. He frowned disapprovingly if she reached for a second helping. When she performed to his specifications, she glowed in his attention. When she didn't, she cowered in his glares.

She became his puppet, dangling this way and that to meet his every whim. But he was seldom satisfied. There was always one more demand. He was only doing it for her good, he said. A self-improvement plan. The problem: it was his plan, not hers! A modern "My Fair Lady" scheme, with his wife the pawn that brought him recognition.

When she was confronted with the question, "Why don't you leave him?" she replied, "It's tough to live alone, being a single parent is difficult, and he does make a decent living!"

"Do you love him?"

"No," she answered without hesitation. "I don't. How can I love someone who can't accept me the way I am?"

The amazing fact is that she could only see his faults, when she herself was far from blameless. While he was using her to meet his need for control and recognition, she was using him to meet her need for comfort and companionship. Neither accepted nor truly loved the other. "Selfish love," we might call it—but in reality it's not really love at all. "Selfish attachment" might be a more accurate term. Both were in the relationship merely to get what they could from the other. The commitment was not "till death do us part," but "till you cease to give me what I need."

Many people live in relationships steeped with conditions, each using and manipulating the other to meet their own needs. Each marching to the other's tune—never fully free to be themselves. Each slaves to the acceptance they crave from the other.

Don't misuse the power of acceptance. If you love unconditionally, your loved ones can experience the freedom of being truly accepted and of being truly themselves. They will never feel used or abused.

Being open and honest

The need for acceptance is often so strong that it is difficult to be open and honest with your loved ones. What about your spotted past? Would they still love you? What about your doubts and dreams? Would they laugh at you? For many, self-disclosure is hardly worth the risk. It is better to keep out of sight the darker parts of our lives rather than risk the rejection of a loved one. But we pay the price. We can never be fully ourselves. We can never feel truly comfortable. We can never feel really accepted as long as we must hide part of ourselves. This leads further to isolation, conflict, and empty love cups.

The wife of a dentist once told me how her husband grew distant as he immersed himself in the task of setting up a new practice. She knew something was bothering him. Each time she asked, she was met with coldness and hostility. At first he was quiet, not speaking much at home. Later he retreated to his study. He ignored the children and her. After some weeks, their communication was at a minimum. In time, he refused to sleep with her. All this time she had no inkling of what was the matter. She didn't know if she had offended him, if he was in financial difficulty, in trouble with the law, having an affair, or ill with a disease. Maybe he was losing his mind. Maybe she was losing hers.

At last she could take it no longer. She overcame her gentle nature to force a confrontation. She yelled, "I can't take this any longer. Tell me what's wrong, or I'm leaving!"

With this, her strong, tall husband sat down, buried his head in his hands, and began to sob. "The practice is going poorly," he admitted. "I'm afraid we won't be able to go on the long vacation we planned."

That was it, nothing more. A trivial matter by any standards. But he couldn't bear to tell her because he was afraid she would not accept him if he couldn't provide what he had promised.

The wife heaved a sigh of relief and said she truly preferred to stay home all summer and tend the garden. But she hadn't said so because she was afraid to disappoint him since he had been looking forward to the trip. Months of misery could have been avoided if each had felt sufficiently accepted to confide in the other.

Paul Tournier in his classic, *To Understand Each Other*, talks about the fear that men often have of sharing their negative emotional selves with their wives. Feelings of bitterness, envy, rejection, or discouragement are not something to be proud of. They rationalize that to share their ugly emotions would cause their wives to think less of them. So craving acceptance, they attempt to bury feelings. They withhold the very part of their lives, that, if shared, would lead to greater intimacy.

Acceptance and the attitude toward authority

Being loved conditionally can affect one's attitude toward authority. As part of his doctoral program at The Claremont Colleges School of Theology, Fred Osborne conducted research on students attending a religious university. He found that a number of students were hostile toward the university and its sponsoring church. Searching the data to discover why, he found that students who were hostile usually felt their own parents' love was conditional. A love which was earned by being polite, getting good grades, wearing decent clothes, making beds, and the like. Non-hostile students tended to feel their parents loved them unconditionally—no matter what they did.

How does conditional love lead to hostility toward authority? One possible explanation of the dynamics: when the students were young and their parents provoked them by their anger, criticism, restrictiveness, or disappointment, they, as children, did not feel free to express their feelings. If they yelled, "I hate it when you treat me like that," or "You make me mad," love might be withdrawn. Children crave acceptance and approval. Most will do anything rather than risk rejection. Therefore, instead of resolving their negative emotions, they harbored them. And with each conflict, the hostile feelings grew.

When hostile feelings become overwhelming, one of two things will happen. Either the children will explode and rebel against their parents, or the hostility is displaced to other "safer" authority figures—people or institutions whose acceptance matters less than parental love and acceptance.

I wonder how the perception of conditional love might affect a child's relationship to God. There is a danger that he or she might perceive that God loves him or her conditionally, as do the parents. The result is too often hostility and rejection toward God. The way parents love, therefore, can affect a child's relationship with God. A heavy responsibility to bear!

If the investigators were to ask each of the parents, "Did you really love your child conditionally?" I'm sure the majority would say, "Of course not. We loved our child all the time, no matter what."

It's not how *you* love, that's important. You might love unconditionally, but if the child thinks he or she is loved conditionally, that perception is what will guide the life. Hence, parents must be sure that the child gets the right message.

What gets in the way of children, family members, or friends getting the message that they're accepted regardless of what they do? It's your anger, criticism, restrictiveness, and disappointment. It happens in marriage too.

I'm reminded of one of King Solomon's truisms:

"A continual dripping on a very rainy day
And a contentious woman are alike"
(Proverbs 27:15).

And then this wise man admits:

"Better to dwell in the wilderness,
Than with a contentious and angry woman"
(Proverbs 21:19).

She is just trying to help her husband become a better person and make sure he won't embarrass her in public. "Honey, your tie is crooked." "Sweetheart, please! Not brown shoes with grey slacks." "You're slurping again." "Don't interrupt." Drip. Drip. Drip.

He takes it for a year or two, maybe twenty, but just as surely as a drip, drip, drip over years begins to make a depression in granite, so does the drip, drip, drip of criticism on a marriage. And love begins to round the bend to the opposite extreme. Twenty-five years after their storybook honeymoon, she's shocked to hear him say, "I don't love you any more. I want out! In fact, I don't think I ever really loved you!"

She queries, "All those endearing words and actions when we were first married, what do you mean you never loved me?" What he's really saying is that he can't remember a time when *he* really felt loved. Why? The anger, criticism, restrictive control, and disappointment: drip, drip, drip. At first he tried to win her acceptance by being the devoted, doting husband, but in the end his weary psyche gives in to his perception: "I'm only loved when I do what she wants." And love turns to hostility.

I've counseled troubled marriages. I've seen couples work through incredible problems: adultery, handicap, chronic illness, prison. But when love turns to hostility caused by the continuous dripping of a contentious wife—or husband—it's almost impossible to reverse the damage.

How anger, criticism, restrictiveness and disappointment empty love cups

Jessica was an ideal child by everyone's standards. She did everything her folks wanted her to do; she was responsible, talented, and smart. A kind, thoughtful, sensitive child who always wanted to please. She got good grades, stayed out of trouble, was a school leader, and her family and friends could always depend on her. Her folks adored her, teachers loved her, and her peers looked up to her. She studied her Bible daily, sang in the choir, and spent a summer in Europe as a student missionary. And then as Jessica was nearing her eighteenth birthday, she began to grow distant, and her bubbly personality burst into one of confusion and sadness. "How can God really love me?" she questioned. She had tried so hard to be good; she was getting tired of the pressure. Regardless of how good she was, she questioned whether it was good enough!

This was the first indication that something was amiss. Over the next few years, with professional help, the pieces began to come together. Jessica's folks loved her dearly and told her often. But their high expectations for her, coupled with just enough anger, criticism, restrictive control, and disappointment to guarantee obedience, was enough for

Jessica to feel their love was conditional on her performance.

Jessica's parents never threatened, "If you don't do this, we'll stop loving you." They never bribed, "If you are elected president of the student body, we'll buy you a car." They never knowingly pushed, shoved, or manipulated. Instead, based on her faulty perception, she pushed herself. Even as an eighth-grader, she checked a book out of the library on the perfectionist personality to try to understand the force within that was driving her. With her bright, analytical mind she began to reason that unconditional love was too good to be true. How could someone be loved merely because she existed? She began to believe, "I've got to do what my folks want, or they won't love me." And she did for eighteen years.

Not every child in a family is at the same degree of risk for misperceiving the basis of parental love. In fact, Jessica's siblings never doubted their folks' unconditional love. They never saw their parents' actions as manipulative. They had different personalities. They felt free to express their own opinions. A raised voice, a correction, a restriction, a sigh of disappointment just rolled off their backs, like water off a duck. But this highly sensitive firstborn, craving her parents' approval, blindly obeyed out of fear of losing their love if she would march to the tune of a different drummer. Not until she was grown was she able to confront her folks, feel confident enough to test their love, and thus free herself of the control she had felt through the growing years by having to perform to their ever-expanding expectations. The control she felt was something her folks had not intended, nor had they even been aware that it existed.

Dennis Guernsey, in his book *The Family Covenant*, gives an illustration of a situation that was similar to what Jessica experienced with her folks. One day Sheryl said to her dad,

"You know, Dad, living with you is like competing in a high jump. Sometimes I get out there and you say, 'Sheryl, here's the standard. Go for it.' Then I run out into whatever I'm doing, and I stand at the side of the high jumping pit. Then I approach the bar and leap over it, and more often than not, I clear it. When I do, you're one of the most enthusiastic and excited cheerleaders in the world.

" 'You did it! You made it! That's great,' you exclaim.

"Then, Dad, you say, 'Now we're going to move the standard up one more inch.'

"It's as if life with you is always one inch higher than I can reach."

As the bar of approval was being raised, the chance of success diminished. Inevitably, the bar would be raised so high that it would be beyond Sheryl's abilities, and she would fail.

If only Jessica had been able to paint a word picture like this so her folks might have understood how their behavior, although well intended, was hurting her.

I tell you this story to impress you with the fact that unconditional love or acceptance is not something we necessarily do or don't do. Control is not necessarily a conscious act. It is basically in the eye of the recipient. You may think you are giving unconditional love, but if your children, your spouse, your friends, or your employees, because of their compliant personalities and sensitive natures, feel controlled by your anger, criticism, restrictiveness, or disappointment, *you* must be the one who changes, or you risk alienation and the consequences of empty love cups.

How can you make sure your family feels loved unconditionally?

Say "I love you" in words and actions. Don't assume your family knows or is convinced of the fact of your love. Make this your motto: "Do not withhold good from those to whom it is due, when it is in the power of your hand to do so" (Proverbs 3:27). And in addition, follow these guidelines:

1. Control your anger. Learn ways of coping with your anger so it doesn't become frightening or abusive to your family. Don't resort to anger to get people to do things just because it works. This is a control mechanism, and control is abusive! Learn how to recognize the first signs that anger is lodging in your heart, and call a spade, a spade. Say, "I'm angry," and shrink that giant. (You'll learn how in the next chapter.) And when you do lose your cool, apologize and clarify with your loved ones that your behavior had nothing to do with your love for them. You love them just because they exist, and you always will!

2. Stop your criticism. Don't excuse yourself by calling it "constructive criticism." It seldom is! Criticism is demeaning. It causes discouragement and low self-worth. And over time, it can turn feelings of love into hostility. Instead, up the praise. Catch people doing good things. Make sure you give your family and friends generous amounts of compliments, pleasant looks, smiles, meaningful touches, and words of encouragement.

3. Lighten up your restrictive nature. You don't have to run the world—or the lives of your family and friends. You don't have to tell them what to do. Demanding, commanding, dictating, and bossing people around empties love cups. Learn to say "Yes" instead of "No" whenever possible. Instead of giving them your opinion, learn to say, "How do you feel about that? What do you think?" Cut your advice in half, or quarter it, and listen twice as much. Learn how to become a persuasive person, not a pushy one. And when you're dying to give them a piece of your mind—ask permission, "Would you like to hear how I feel about the subject?" You might end up giving less of your good advice away, and the people may instead have to learn from their own mistakes, but if in the process they truly feel loved unconditionally, loved irrationally, accepted just the way they are, isn't it worth it?

4. Monitor your expressions of disappointment. Make sure your expectations of others are realistic. Clarify that your acceptance of them is not performance-based. Their goals should be for personal satisfaction, not yours. People, especially children, crave approval, and, for some, a look of disappointment, a deep sigh, a shake of the head, or a frown from a significant person is a painful wound. It signals disapproval; failure. Don't let your own standards get in the way of a love-based relationship.

Especially for self-driven, perfectionistic people, you must learn to validate their feelings of failure or shame, rather than express your own. And tag your comments with a performance-based disclaimer statement. For example. "You feel you've let me down by. . . . But I want you to know I'll always love you just because you're you, not for what you do or don't do. In my eyes you'll always be a winner."

This must be our message:

> "I'll love you forever, I'll like you for always.
> "As long as I'm living, my baby,
> (child, friend, lover) you'll be."
> (From Robert Munsch's picture book,
> *Love You Forever*).

Chapter Eight

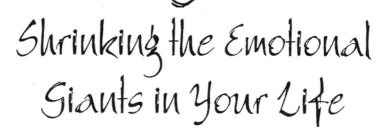

Shrinking the Emotional Giants in Your Life

"Great giants work great wrongs—but we are small.
For love goes lowly; but oppressions tall."
—*Thomas Hood*

Negative emotions are the biggest single factor that threatens the safe delivery of the unconditional acceptance message. When you're boiling inside, you can't *care* for others' needs with the type of tenderness that communicates love. When you hate the things a person is doing and feel persecuted and used, it's impossible to treat that person with *respect.* How can you *forgive* when you're harboring resentment, bitterness, and revenge? And it's easy to substitute control for *trust*, just to show an offensive person who is in charge! It's tough to fill the love cup of a person who has just made you so angry that you feel like screaming! It's impossible to conduct a loving conversation with someone who incites you to jealousy, fear, shame, or revenge.

Negative emotions are the underlying cause of our inability to control our anger, stop the criticism, lighten up on our restrictive natures, and show approval rather than disappointment, which are the four major reasons people don't feel accepted and loved.

So, if you want to be skilled in filling love cups, it's important to learn how to handle emotional giants—those negative emotions in your life.

You don't have to be a giant-killer; just learn how to cut them down to size so problems can be solved in a rational manner. Negative emotions serve a very important function. When you are in danger, your reflex response is fear; it prepares you to flee, to fight, or to avoid greater danger. When someone mistreats you, anger is the emotion that may motivate you to a solution. When you have wronged someone, guilt helps you say, "I'm sorry," and seek restitution. But when you ignore negative emotions, they grow out of proportion and become like giants, controlling you, causing you or others to feel demeaned, hurt, or shameful.

Emotional giants can be suppressed, but they're too big to bury and keep hidden for long. They keep growing and force their way back to the surface. Sometimes they seem to break out in an explosion. Other times they surface slowly. But regardless, negative emotions not expressed in words usually end up being negative emotions expressed in actions guaranteed to hurt others.

Here is a small example of a giant emotion: Imagine that your husband fails to kiss you before leaving for work. You feel unhappy and hurt as you watch him get into the car and back down the driveway. But you say nothing; you do nothing. As the day wears on, you remember that he didn't kiss you the day before. You grumble to yourself, "What's happening to our marriage? He's beginning to take me for granted. He doesn't need a wife. All he needs is a servant to fix supper and mend his socks." Your hurt feeling grows. You usually call him at lunch time, but not today; let him call you. Noon comes and goes, and no call. You're getting furious. "How can he treat me like this?" you ask. "If this is all the attention he gives me, I'll show him! I won't even cook supper tonight!"

What's happening? An inconsequential event has mushroomed into an ugly giant filled with unhappiness, hurt, anger, and revenge. Finally, you decide to withdraw. In your anger you choose not to be home when he arrives. You go out and squander his paycheck, buying things for yourself. "It serves him right," you say. "Maybe this will teach him he can't take me for granted."

When a person feels taken advantage of, hurt, or used, the natural tendency is revenge. I once saw a cartoon of a husband and wife arguing at the beginning of the day. It then pictured the husband coming home after work with a bouquet of roses, calling to his wife, "Sweetheart, are you still angry?" And there at his place on the kitchen table, was an open can of dog food! I laughed, and when I tell others about the cartoon, they do too. Why? Because we've all experienced that feeling of wanting to get back at someone who has wronged us. I just hope you never resort to dog food!

Revenge comes without thinking—a spontaneous act to treat others as we have been treated. But that's not scriptural. The Golden Rule is to treat others *as we would like* to be treated, not *as we have been* treated!

Negative emotions might be considered positive for about thirty seconds. That's enough time to realize you're experiencing an uncomfortable feeling and choose to do something about it so it won't continue to grow.

Put yourself into the pretend picture once again. What should you do if your husband forgets to kiss you? Perhaps you could dash out of the house and run down the driveway calling, "Honey, give me a kiss! I'm going to feel hurt without a proper farewell." Almost surely he would stop the car, come back, and give you a memorable kiss. Even a better one than the average. Why? Because the neighbors are watching? No, because you chose to communicate how you were feeling and made him aware of your empty cup. Your willingness to share gave him the opportunity to respond in love and fill you up.

There are other ways of letting a spouse know you're empty, if sprinting down driveways isn't your style. Perhaps you could call him at work and tell him you'll take a long-distance kiss over the phone in expectation of the real thing when he gets home. Or a simple note to put with his stack of mail saying, "Roses are red, Violets are blue, This morning I missed my goodbye kiss from you!" The simple fact is, doing something immediately about a negative emotion, frees you from struggling with a growing giant.

You need to learn how to shrink the emotional giants in your life and in the lives of your loved ones. It's a must. Consistent, loving communication with your family and friends depends on it.

There are three major giant-shrinking techniques that

are important to master: The "I feel" statement to shrink the potential negative emotion giant in your own life. The "you feel" statement when someone else's giant needs shrinking. And in tense situations, try "warm fuzzies." Read on!

The "I feel" giant shrinker

A few simple jingles might help you understand the giants in your life and how to effectively shrink them. To start:

> Straight talk is what you do
> If there's no giant in them or you.

If there's no underlying emotions there is no problem. You're talking straight. Without fear of upset, you can objectively discuss home finances, tuition costs, solar heating, or anything else. With disagreement, however, emotions often flare. Perhaps the other person is not listening. The giant starts growing. The trouble begins when you raise your voice or feel like stomping your feet. If you don't act quickly to shrink your giant, it is likely to control you. The technique to use is a simple "I feel" statement before you end up acting out the emotion in hurtful ways.

> To shrink the giant in your life
> An "I feel" statement saves you strife.

Here is the anatomy of an "I feel" statement. It has three parts: "I feel," "when," and "because." Now, let's put it all together.

Begin with "I feel" and clearly state the emotion you feel. The more specific the better. To help you grab the feeling that's grabbing you, read down through the following list of troublesome emotions.

Negative Emotions

abhorrence, aggressive, agitated, alienated, anger, annoyance, antagonism, apathy, anxiety, bashful, belligerence, bitter, bored, brokenhearted, cautious, concerned, condemned, confused, crazy, crotchety, defeated, defensive, defiant, degraded, dejected, deluded, demeaned, depressed, despair, despised, despondent, detached, determined, devastated, disappointed, disapproving, disbelieving, discomforted, discontented, discouraged, disdainful, disgraced, disgruntled, disgusted, dishonorable, disintegrated, disloyal, disorganized, dissatisfied, distraught, distressed, downtrodden, embarrassed, embittered, embroiled, enraged, envious, exasperated, explosive, fanatical, fatalistic, fearful, fiendish, flaky, foreboding, frightened, frigid, frugal, frustrated, furious, gloomy, greedy, grudging, grumpy, guilty, hateful, haughty, heartbroken, homely, homesick, hopeless, hostile, humiliated, hurt, hysterical, idealistic, impatient, inadequate, incompetent, indifferent, insatiable, insecure, insolent, intimidated, intolerant, introverted, irrational, irritated, jealous, lethargic, lonely, martyred, mettlesome, mischievous, miserable, moody, morbid, morose, objectionable, oppressed, outraged, overwhelmed, parsimonious, perplexed, pity, pugnacious, prudish, rage, remorse, repelled, repentant, repressed, resentment, revengeful, sad, shamed, sheepish, shocked, skeptical, smug, somber, sorrowful, spiteful, suspicious, tempted, terrorized, tired, tormented, touchy, tyrannical, undecided, unwanted, vain, valueless, vengeful, victimized, violated, withdrawn, worried, worthless.

You probably had no idea there were so many negative

emotions that could harass you. But let's chose a common one, like anxious. Your "I feel" statement would start with the words, "I feel anxious."

Next, add "when" followed by the situation that has aroused the emotion. The statement might now read, "I feel anxious when you don't let me know when you'll be home late."

But that's not all.

"Because" is next, followed by the reason for your feeling. "because I don't want anything to happen to you."

The complete "I feel" statement would sound like this: "I feel anxious when you don't let me know if you'll be home late, because I don't want anything to happen to you."

Here are some other "I feel" statements.

"I feel used when no one helps me with the dishes, because I don't like to work alone."

"I feel angry when I hear rumors that you've said things about me, because I value my reputation."

"I feel anxious when I get home from work and there is no message telling me where you are, because I think you might have been in an accident."

These statements are called confrontive "I feel" statements, because you confront the person who has caused the situation that has aroused your emotion. Now in theory, when you confront your children with, "I feel angry when no one helps me wash the car . . ." they are supposed to say, "I had no idea you felt this way, Mom. We'll come immediately and help." In theory that's what is supposed to happen! But just in case it doesn't, your statement has not been in vain. It has done something for you. Because you expressed your feeling, you don't have to continue harboring a growing negative emotion.

You've gotten it out on the table and can then discuss with your family what steps need to be taken so the problem can be solved.

It's time to practice. But a word of caution. "I feel" must be followed by the emotion, not by the word "that." If you say "I feel that," you are giving an opinion and not expressing an emotion. Are you ready?

• Every morning your daughter dashes off to school leaving the bathroom a mess. You've had it and decide it's time for a confrontive "I feel" statement.

Fill in the blanks:

I feel _____

when _____

because _____

• Your four-year-old niece is teasing the dog again, pulling its tail. What would you say?

I feel

when

because

• Your wife tosses the clean laundry in a basket after it is dried and by the time you get around to hanging up your clothes, everything is wrinkled. Instead of criticizing and risking her retort, "Next time you can wash your own clothes!" say,

I feel _____

when _____

because _____

• Your friend has a habit of popping in on you when you're not expecting company and your place is a mess. What would you say?

I feel _____

when _____

because _____

At first this may sound a little stilted, but once it becomes a habit, you'll find yourself comfortably clearing the air as needed.

But, you say, this doesn't solve anything. It just brings up the problem. That's not true. It solves the problem of your growing emotion. Your children may not rush into the kitchen and start washing the dishes, but at least you don't have to fuss and fume over their inconsiderateness, until when one of them innocently asks, "Mom, how do you spell encyclopedia?" you explode, "Why should I help you when you haven't helped me?"

Explosions, like volcanic eruptions, cause hurt, misunderstandings, and pain. Granted, an explosion is one way to bring the problem up for discussion, but why go this route, when there is a pain-free, safe, and faster course you can take? A prompt "I feel" statement.

Taking the "I feel" route leads to faster problem solving. You can't effectively deal with problems if there are too many negative emotions interfering with your relationship. Before you can think clearly about a solution that won't be tinged with revenge, guilt, or some other negative emotion, those emotions must be dealt with; shrunk down to problem-solving size!

Not all negative emotions need to be solved by a confrontive "I feel" statement to the offending person. The person might not be available, or your feelings may be irrational and would only cause the other pain. Sometimes you may not know what's causing your painful feelings. There are two variations on the "I feel" statement which may prove helpful in these situations.

First, write your feelings down. "I feel . . ." and continue pouring them out on the paper. As you write, as you begin to transfer those feelings from the confusion in the pit of your stomach to the paper, you will begin to think more clearly. The giant will begin to shrink. Ideas may come to you about what to do next. You may decide your feelings are irrational and what you need to do is play a hard game of tennis, clean the garage, get a good night's sleep, or take a couple days off and regroup! If someone has offended you, and you feel it would not solve anything to confront the offender personally, write it down. Pour all your negative feelings into your "I feel" letter. You'll begin to feel better. Just don't send it! Read it over again, add to it if the feeling persists, and when you begin to feel a release from the giant's hold, burn it!

Second, tell God an "I feel" statement. Tell Him exactly

how you are feeling. You might even blame Him for what's happening in your life. Tell Him. Others have, and God's shoulders have been broad enough to take it. In fact, King David was good at giving God "I feel" statements—his Psalms are full of them. And God never resented David spilling out his guts to Him. In fact, David was so intimate with God in sharing his every emotion, and so open in repentance, that God called him "a man after my own heart." Psalm 38 is a great example. You can't get much lower with the strangle hold of depression than this!

O LORD, do not rebuke me in Your wrath,
Nor chasten me in Your hot displeasure!
For Your arrows pierce me deeply,
And Your hand presses me down.
There is no soundness in my flesh
Because of Your anger,
Nor is there any health in my bones
Because of my sin.
For my iniquities have gone over my head;
Like a heavy burden they are too heavy for me.
My wounds are foul and festering
Because of my foolishness.
I am troubled, I am bowed down greatly;
I go mourning all the day long.
For my loins are full of inflammation,
And there is no soundness in my flesh.
I am feeble and severely broken;
I groan because of the turmoil of my heart.
Lord, all my desire is before You;
And my sighing is not hidden from You.
My heart pants, my strength fails me;

As for the light of my eyes, it also has gone from me.

My loved ones and my friends stand aloof from my plague,

And my kinsmen stand afar off.

Those also who seek my life lay snares for me;

Those who seek my hurt speak of destruction,

And plan deception all the day long.

But I, like a deaf man, do not hear;

And I am like a mute who does not open his mouth.

Thus I am like a man who does not hear,

And in whose mouth is no response (Psalm 38:1-14).

David was pretty low, wasn't he? But notice what happened when he got it all out in the open. It's as if he gets to the end of the road, makes a turn, and begins his journey back to emotional health.

For in You, O LORD, I hope;

You will hear, O Lord my God. . . .

Do not forsake me, O LORD;

O my God, be not far from me!

Make haste to help me,

O Lord, my salvation! (Psalm 38:15, 22).

"I feel" statements provide a means to communicate frankly with God, our loved ones, or associates. It's a way to let them know clearly what's going on inside—both the negative and the positive.

The "I feel" *negative* statement shrinks the giant troublesome emotions in your own self, allowing you to be a better cup filler. The "I feel" *positive* statements work like a protective sealer on your personal love cup to keep it from leaking during the day. An "I feel" positive statement expands positive emotions. Remember, there's only so much room in your cup. If it's filled with the positive, the negative won't have much of a chance to invade. But if the negative is allowed entrance, these heavy emotions sink to the bottom and start to expand, leaving precious little or no room for the positive.

There are so many wonderful positive feelings—too many to list. But to just get started, perhaps you feel . . . accepted, adored, alive, amorous, blissful, competent, confident, contented, demure, forgiven, esteemed, excited, generous, happy, humorous, idealistic, interested, joyful, loved, passionate, pleased, relaxed, relieved, respected, satisfied, thankful, thoughtful, or trusted.

Start your day with a positive "I feel" statement to God in order to protect your cup from the negative invaders. "Lord, I feel thankful when I wake up in the morning to the sunshine and realize all the blessings You have provided for me, because I love sunny days."

Then turn to your family. Fill them up with positive "I feel" statements:

- "I feel happy when you fill the gas tank because it saves me time and I'm off to a quick start."
- "I feel joyful when you practice without being reminded because soon you'll be playing so well, you'll find joy in your music too."
- "I feel relieved when I come home to a clean house because I enjoy spending time with you rather than spending time cleaning."

· · · · · **115**

The more expressions of positive emotion, the more resistant your cup will be to troublesome emotions. So, when your emotion is happiness, joy, or relief, express it!

The "you feel" giant shrinker

The complement of "I feel" is "you feel." A "you feel" statement is used to deal with someone else's emotion. It's incredible the love-cup power you can have over the emotions of others. The motto to remember is:

> When the giant's curve is thrown your way,
> A "you feel" statement is what to say.

When someone gives vent to an underlying emotion, you can respond with a "you feel" statement of clarification and shrink their giant. Examples calling for such a response: "I hate my teacher." "I never again want to walk home alone." "You're always buying something for yourself and never for me."

The emotion must first be dealt with in order to uncover the person's underlying meaning. A "you feel" statement can help to do this. It's a clarifying statement. With this technique you can validate the person's feelings without being threatening. It's impossible to solve problems when emotional giants are sparring with one another. Once you have defused the other's giant with "you feel," you can continue listening until you uncover the real problem.

Negative behavior is like the tip of an iceberg. It's the part we clearly see: behaviors such as stomping feet, throwing things, yelling, crying, sassing, blaming, slamming doors, or pouting. But what you see is not the entire iceberg. The largest mass is beneath the surface of the water. That's true with negative emotions. Whenever you see negative behavior, you know there is something under the surface that is causing this behavior. To chip away at the top of the iceberg, trying to get rid of the behavior you don't like, won't solve the problem. It may chip off some pieces of the iceberg, but the iceberg will right itself and something else will stick out. The only way to get rid of an iceberg, is to melt it!

So it is with negative emotions. If you get angry enough and threaten you might get rid of the negative behavior for a time, but it won't solve the underlying problem causing this behavior. Until you deal with anger, frustration, fear, embarrassment, or whatever the aggravating emotion is, there is a good chance another negative behavior will surface.

At one of my seminars a mother related a typical iceberg tale: Her young son sassed her. She threatened, spanked, and ended up washing out his mouth with soap. She stopped the sassing. Later that day she began dressing to go shopping. She opened her pantyhose drawer and pulled out a pair. The legs had been cut off! She tried another. The same thing. Her son had gone through the whole drawer of pantyhose cutting off the legs. The moral: Unless you get to the bottom of the problem, the negative emotion that is causing the negative behavior, the problem isn't really solved. And beware, the secondary expression of negative behavior may be worse than the first!

That's why the "you feel" clarifying statement is so important. For a moment you ignore the negative behavior. You reach for the negative emotions and allow the person plagued with the emotion to express the emotion in words. This shrinks the emotion; defuses it. The negative behavior melts away. Once the emotion has been dealt with, then the person can think more clearly about how the problem can be solved.

Your part as a giant shrinker is merely to say, "You feel _____" (supply the negative emotion) and LISTEN! I can't stress this enough. Your tendency will be to give information immediately. "Oh, you feel angry; you should pay him back by doing something nice for him." That is the wrong thing to do! Even though your wise counsel may be exactly what the person should do, by your giving this information prematurely you sabotage the giant shrinking process. Trust the process. It works! Say, "You feel _____" and LISTEN. It takes time for giant negative emotions to shrink. But in time they will, and then you can ask, "What do you think you might do to solve the problem?" The chance is great that the person will ask, "What do you think I should do?" That is the invitation for information.

If you feel the person needs to learn a more appropriate way of expressing his or her emotions than through their negative behavior, the time to instruct is after the problem is solved. If you try too early, you'll only arouse more negative emotion and the whole process will grind to a halt.

The "you feel" statement does not always have to be said in those exact words. It must be initiated with, "you feel," when it's important to clarify the feeling, but as the person with the giant emotion begins to share, you don't want to sound like a robot. "Oh, you feel sad. You feel jealous. You feel guilty. You feel . . ." When that happens "you feel" becomes merely a sterile technique, devoid of real interest and concern for the other. Since the defusing of giant emotions takes listening time, you'll want to learn other methods to encourage further sharing and clarifying. You can ask, "Tell me more . . ." You can use staccato expressions of empathy. "That's tough!" "It really hurt you, didn't it!" "It's frustrating when things like that happen." Use as few words as possible. Remember, the giant only shrinks when the person with the giant is talking! That's why one-syllable expressions of continued interest work so well, "Oh; Yes; Ummm; Yah; No; My." It's just enough to let the person know that he or she has your complete attention. Let your body language say; "I'm listening." Lean forward; look interested; maintain eye contact; open your arms rather than cross them, which is a closed position; and don't, *please don't*, look at your watch!

Now let's set the stage for an iceberg behavior that desperately needs a "you feel" clarifying statement.

Your husband slams down the phone and shouts; "I can't believe it. I feel like marching right over and giving him a piece of my mind. How could he tell me one thing and do exactly the opposite. See if I'll ever invite him again. I've had it!" he says as he sweeps his arm across the table, sending the newspaper flying."

You're tempted to give information and zero in on the tip of the iceberg. "Honey, that's no way to act. You shouldn't say those things. And look what you've done to the paper!" Bite your tongue! Think iceberg! And immediately form a simple three-word giant shrinker, "You feel . . . angry!" Then stop and listen. You'll be surprised at the power you have to shrink the emotions in others.

The "warm fuzzy" giant shrinker

How do you respond to people who try to put you down with malice or spite? They usually have a giant negative emotion that is moving them to action. They may be terribly upset, beyond the reach of a "you feel" statement. So you must try something else to shrink the giant:

If you feel put down by a giant's attack;
Send warm fuzzies and you'll pay him back.

Creating Love

Warm fuzzies is a term often used for compliments, words of appreciation, or kind acts. To an agitated person, warm fuzzies work like shock therapy. A warm fuzzy is the last thing an angry person expects. It disarms him or her and often defuses an explosive situation.

It may not cut the giant down to size, but it keeps the giant from growing larger. It's also a great protection against letting your own giant grow in response to a put-down. Warm fuzzies are great love cup fillers.

You come home late and your wife has been waiting with supper. This is the third night in a row. Her patience runs out. She's angry and yells, "Why can't you be home on time?"

You know she's mad. And your excuse is poor. You could try a "you feel" statement to her towering giant, "Wow; honey, you feel angry . . ." but it would probably sound like a put-down and make her even more furious. So try some warm fuzzies. You've got nothing to lose.

You might say, "I appreciate your having a great supper ready for me. You're a super wife!" "Supper smells scrumptious, and since you've worked so hard, I'll be happy to do the dishes tonight." Then you should add, "By the way, I'm sure sorry. I lost track of time. I'll try to be more careful. I know how you feel. Forgive me.'"

It's a calloused wife who wouldn't forgive a husband after that recital. Some wives would nearly faint. After the fuzzies do their love-cup-filling job, you can do some problem-solving without those emotional giants getting in the way.

Teach your children to throw warm fuzzies instead of becoming defensive. Robert Schuller tells the story of a little girl who went shopping with her daddy during the Christmas season. They had little money, so Dad was trying hard to scrimp and save. He wasn't paying much attention as the

120 · · · ·

items were being checked by the cashier. It was not until he got home that he noticed his daughter had put a package of expensive gold wrapping paper into their cart. His anger flared; he ripped into his daughter with hurtful words and then stomped off to the other room. Later, deciding to return the paper, he went to look for it. When he couldn't find it, he called to his daughter and asked her to bring the gold wrapping paper to him. "OK, Daddy," she replied in a cheerful tone. A few minutes later she brought him a big box wrapped in the expensive gold paper. He exploded. Not only had she purchased the paper, but now she had used it so it couldn't be returned. Wasted! After his tirade, the girl urged, "Daddy, open your present. It's for you." Reluctantly he opened the big box. It was empty. Once more his frustration got the most of him. "Why did you waste that expensive paper wrapping an empty box? When you give a present there should at least be something in it!"

"But, Daddy," she exclaimed. "There is something in the box. Before I wrapped it I blew kisses into the box. The box is filled with kisses for you."

Now tell me, what father's giant emotion, even a persistent one, wouldn't burst with a warm fuzzy like that!

If you wonder about the warm fuzzies, and whether it's not a contrived idea to "suck-up" to a person for your own benefit, ponder Proverbs 25:21-22. Warm fuzzies are merely an application of the biblical admonition, "If an enemy is hungry, give him food. If he is thirsty, give him drink—for you shall be heaping coals of fire on his head." *The Living Bible* reads, "This will make him feel ashamed of himself." In other words, when you do this good turn for evil, the person is so embarrassed that his face turns red as if coals of fire were heaped on his head!

Creating Love

If a fuzzy is good treatment for an enemy, it might even be better for a loved one: your child, husband, wife, parent or friend. It's a strong sign of acceptance.

I always welcome warm fuzzies, I'd like to get one right now. That's one nice thing about warm fuzzies, you don't have to wait for those giants to appear to throw them! But when you spot a giant coming your way, you can't afford to procrastinate. Throw some warm fuzzies quickly. Fill up that empty person's love cup and see if it doesn't make a difference. Remember, only when a love cup is full to overflowing is there enough love to give away.

Chapter Nine

Forgiveness—
Love's Toughest Work

"Forgiving is love's toughest work,
and love's biggest risk."
—*Lewis B. Smedes*

When my dad was the owner of a fishing tackle manufacturing business, he had to take trips across the country to find wholesale outlets for his products. I remember he always brought us kids something when he returned: a bag of peanuts, balloons, or trinkets he had picked up at a convention. One time he brought us a kaleidoscope. What a wonderful thing. With just a twist the world would take on a different look, an endless variety. Out of curiosity I pried the end off and was disappointed to find only a few broken pieces of colored glass. But held to the light, that kaleidoscope transferred them into something beautiful and whole.

Forgiveness is a kaleidoscope for broken relationships. It takes hurt, anger, fear, misunderstanding, shame, embarrassment, pride, and guilt and gives us a new perspective on them. It makes something beautiful out of the ugly pieces of our lives. Extending and accepting forgiveness, which bridges the chasm of alienation, creating a new positive-energy relationship, is perhaps as close as we can come to experiencing the transforming power of God's creative love.

But forgiving, although easy to talk about, is hard to do, because it demands selflessness. It strips us of defenses we've built to protect our egos. It destroys platforms we have erected to make us look better or feel superior to others. When forgiveness is either graciously given or courageously asked for, we are reduced to square one: we are all sinners and in need of forgiveness. We are no better than the worst. We all make mistakes that unless rectified, produce the cancer of hate that eats away our lives. The need for forgiveness is a serious matter.

And in no other area of love are the consequences of omission or commission so poignant. With our greatest desire being life eternal and knowing the door to that opportunity hinges on God's forgiveness, we are reminded that His forgiveness is conditional. At first this seems in juxtaposition to God's unconditional love, but in reality it supports it. God loves us regardless and accepts us just the way we are, but since God cannot condone our sinful behavior, we must be willing to ask forgiveness and grant forgiveness. Every time we repeat the model prayer that Jesus taught us to pray, "And forgive us our debts, as we forgive our debtors," we are reminded that the same forgiveness we desire from God, must be granted by us to others.

Forgiveness—Love's Toughest Work

Forgiveness is an emotional ordinance of humility that prepares us to receive Christ. It's as if there is only so much room in our love cups, and when we retain a corner for bitterness, hatred, revenge, or pride, there is not enough room for God's forgiveness. It requires all space or none. Our act of forgiving others who have hurt us and asking forgiveness from those we have hurt is the Draino that flushes out the most stubborn clogs of negative emotion, allowing God's love to fill us to overflowing.

Forgiveness is at the core of relationship. It removes walls of separation. It breaks down prison bars we've built to protect ourselves from our enemies, and it gives us perfect freedom to experience unconditional love relationships without fear. But it only works if forgiveness is granted or received unconditionally, irrespective of the magnitude of the sin committed against us—or that we have committed. There is one standard for all—forgive and you shall be forgiven. There is no mistake so small that we can overlook the cleansing transaction of forgiveness that must take place. And just to make sure that through the ages we would clearly understand that there are no limits on forgiveness, Jesus told a story. Listen to it again through the eyes of Eugene Peterson's paraphrase of Matthew 18:23-35 in *The Message*:

"The kingdom of God is like a king who decided to square accounts with his servants. As he got under way, one servant was brought before him who had run up a debt of a hundred thousand dollars. He couldn't pay up, so the king ordered the man, along with his wife, children, and goods, to be auctioned off at the slave market.

"The poor wretch threw himself at the king's feet

and begged, 'Give me a chance and I'll pay it all back.' Touched by his plea, the king let him off, erasing the debt.

"The servant was no sooner out of the room when he came upon one of his fellow servants who owed him ten dollars. He seized him by the throat and demanded, 'Pay up. Now!'

"The poor wretch threw himself down and begged, 'Give me a chance and I'll pay it all back.' But he wouldn't do it. He had him arrested and put in jail until the debt was paid. When the other servants saw this going on, they were outraged and brought a detailed report to the king.

"The king summoned the man and said, 'You evil servant! I forgave your entire debt when you begged me for mercy. Shouldn't you be compelled to be merciful to your fellow servant who asked for mercy?' The king was furious and put the screws to the man until he paid back his entire debt. And that's exactly what my Father in heaven is going to do to each one of you who doesn't forgive unconditionally anyone who asks for mercy."

It's pretty clear, isn't it? Forgiveness isn't an option. It's a command!

The basics of forgiveness

But it's such a small thing, do I really need to ask forgiveness? Yes. If you have hurt someone physically, psychologically, spiritually, or materially, regardless of the extent of the injury, that's cause for forgiveness.

But it's such a small thing, do I really need to forgive? Yes. Forgiveness is the only road to reconciliation.

Forgiveness—Love's Toughest Work

But what if the other person doesn't ask to be forgiven? Don't let your forgiveness be conditional on whether or not they ask.

But what if they aren't in the least bit repentant? All you are asked to do is build the bridge on your side of the chasm. Let God worry about the connection.

But what if I don't think I've done anything wrong, and the other person is just too sensitive or is unjustly blaming me? If there is hurt and alienation, there needs to be reconciliation—and the only road to reconciliation is forgiveness. Ask forgiveness for causing the person hurt.

But if I ask forgiveness, won't that be an admission that I was wrong? No. Your action may be justified. The problem is the hurt it caused. If there is hurt and estrangement, there is need of forgiveness and reconciliation.

But what if the law was on my side, and I didn't do anything wrong? The letter of the law may be on your side, but you can be dead right and still kill another with your attitude, manner, and timing. Before painting yourself into the corner of perfection, examine your motives. Were they really lily white? Before pointing out the splinter in another's eye, remove the log in your own.

But if I forgive, won't that give them approval to do it again? You are only responsible for what *you* should do. Don't try to control another by your behavior. God will wrestle with your offenders. But your forgiveness may soften them enough to make God's job easier.

But what if they keep hurting me? How many times should I forgive?

Peter asked that question and thought he was really being magnanimous to suggest perhaps seven times. Jesus' reply however, made it clear that when it comes to forgiveness, there are no limits, "Seven! Hardly. Try seventy times seven." (See Matthew 18:21-22, *The Message*.)

But what if they don't deserve forgiveness? Forgiveness is never deserved. It is always a gift.

But I don't know where the other person is. Make an honest attempt to find the person. If you keep hitting dead ends, write a letter, put a stamp on it in anticipation of finding the location of the person. Then wait for God's timing. You have done your part.

But what if the person is dead? Put your words of forgiveness, or your request for forgiveness on paper. Or go to the grave site, as a symbolic gesture, and speak aloud. Although the other will never know, the miracle of forgiveness will happen in your heart.

But what if the other person doesn't want to have anything more to do with me? Or what if I really don't want anything to do with him or her? There are always consequences to sin. Build your side of the bridge. The consequence is that the other side of the bridge may never be built. Or if both sides are built, that doesn't mean that it will ever be crossed again. The importance of the bridge is that it's there if either ever wants to use it. Forgiveness does not mean the bridge must be used in the future.

But what if I forgive, but still feel hurt and angry? Hurt is not unbearable. And anger is a justified emotion when wronged. What is unbearable is hurt and anger coupled with blame, hate, rage, revenge, and bitterness. Hurt is a consequence of a wound. Anger is a consequence of unfair treatment. These feelings may never be erased entirely. But forgiveness eradicates blame, hate, rage, revenge, and bitterness, which eat away our own health and selfhood and cause us to want to destroy another's. With forgiveness-cushioned time, the hurt and anger will lessen.

But how do you know you've been forgiven? Idealistically, the forgiver and the forgiven will seek reconciliation. Realistically, you may never know. You are only responsible for your own feelings and behavior.

But how do I know if I have really forgiven someone? You will find yourself wishing them the best in life. You can honestly ask the Lord to give them the same blessings you have asked for yourself.

But what if I don't feel like forgiving? Feelings don't necessarily precede actions. The chance is quite high, however, that feelings will follow the act of forgiveness. The biblical principle is, "If you know these things, happy are you if you do them" (John 13:17). Feelings are fickle. Don't count on your feelings as predictable indicators of right action. Forgiveness is an act of your will, not of your feelings.

But what if I can't forgive? What if the wrong done to me is unforgivable? To say "I can't" is just another way of saying, "I won't." "With God all things are possible," (Mark 10:27) including forgiveness. Here are two stories that originally appeared in *Guideposts* that illustrate this fact and document what forgiveness does for the forgiver.

In the first, Elizabeth Morris tells of her impassioned hatred of the drunk driver who killed her eighteen-year-old son. When she saw him in the courtroom the sight sickened her, her hands trembled, and tears ran together beneath her chin. She cried irrationally, "If I ever see him walking across the street, I'll run him down!" The irony of it all was that as Elizabeth screamed for revenge, Tommy Pigage walked free, as charges were reduced and court dates were postponed. He was finally sentenced to five years of probation with alternate weekends to be served in the county jail, but if he broke parole he would begin serving a ten-year term immediately. She was obsessed with catching him violating parole. One day she saw him in front of his house and on an impulse stopped. He'd been drinking. She told him he needed direction in his life and asked if it would be OK if she would send him some Bible study material. To her surprise he nodded yes. She thought, "I'll never forgive him, but at least I can do this."

A few days later Tommy broke parole and was slapped in jail to begin serving the ten-year sentence. Still obsessed with making sure he got what he deserved, she called to check on him and happened to ask if anyone had been to see him. "No one," the parole officer said.

"No one at all?" she exclaimed.

Without thinking she asked if she could visit. When ushered inside, seeing him in the same clothes he'd had on for three days, his shoulders drooping, she softened. But she wasn't prepared for his words, "Mrs. Morris, I'm so sorry. Please forgive me."

Suddenly she saw Tommy, not as the murderer of her son, but as a person in need of love and guidance. And not able to stand it any longer she said, "I forgive you, Tommy. And now I want you to forgive me."

"Why?" he questioned.

"For hating you."

Elizabeth Morris, as she tells her story, says: "And there we were. The drunk driver and the mother of the one he'd killed, feeling the torment begin to fall away. We were free. Both of us" (Elizabeth Morris, "Seventy Times Seven," *Guideposts*, 1985).

The second story is about Hasula Hanna, a widow whose only child Pat was brutally raped and murdered.

Bitterness raged inside her.

Pat's death seemed to affect everything in her life. A small business investment went sour, leaving her angry at herself and at the former friend who had recommended it.

Soon, she was almost a recluse. She turned down invitations to dinner and social affairs. Only the force of habit kept her attending church.

Two years of lonely journeys to the graves of her daughter and husband left her not caring even whether or not her life lasted any longer. She said, "All that seemed alive was the hate burning within me like a subterranean fire in a vein of coal, smoldering, consuming everything in me that had once responded to love, laughter and beauty."

The story ends with Hasula being impressed by God to send a Gideon Bible to the murderer with the message, "Because Jesus forgives her, Mrs. Hanna forgives you, and because Jesus said, 'Love one another,' Mrs. Hanna loves you.'" She said it was as if someone else were saying the words, but as soon as she got home she fell on her bed and cried until there were no more tears. She writes: "I was free. When I had made the gesture of forgiveness with the gift of the Bible, God had removed the rancor and alienation that had burdened my heart for so long."

And as for the murderer? Never before had anyone said they loved him. Her message was a wedge into his hard heart, and he accepted Christ's forgiveness. The influence of his changed life brought many fellow prisoners to the freedom that Christ's forgiveness gives (Hasula Hanna, "My Prison of Hate," *Guideposts*, September, 1982).

You may think the sin against you is unforgivable, but God can place love in your heart, not for what the person did, but for the person.

Creating Love

A personal confession

I want you to see me in the best possible light. A writer, a professional in the area of family relationships, an adoring wife, a competent mother, and what I am going to share next strips away the lovely facade and makes me look very, very human.

You see, although you are reading chapter 9 and still have six more chapters to go before finishing, this is not the order in which the book was written. I just could not get a handle on this thing called forgiveness. And so when I came to forgiveness, I skipped to the area of trust, finished the last chapter of the book, and then went back to fill in the missing chapters on forgiveness. I sat at my computer. I typed words, then deleted. I prayed, still nothing came. My deadline was bearing down on me, yet I seemed empty.

Seldom do I read what others have said on a topic at the time I'm writing. It's too easy to get caught in the delicious phrases of others and become a copy machine rather than totally trusting that God can say something unique through me. But my barrenness forced me to my bookshelf. I pulled down three volumes. *When It's Hard to Forgive* by Goldie Bristol with Carol McGinnis, Dennis B. Guernsey's book *The Family Covenant: Love and Forgiveness*, and the popular *Forgive and Forget* by Lewis B. Smedes.

Perhaps my problem was my inability to identify with the topic. I knew without a doubt that forgiveness was an essential part of love. But, I had never really seen myself as guilty and, therefore, had very little experience in the art.

Being totally honest, sometimes far too honest (or wordy) for my own good, whenever I knowingly make mistakes I own up and get on with life. And I forgive easily. Life has enough burdens—why should I choose to carry around a grudge? And although I know I've made mistakes with my kids, and continue to, they are open enough to let me know when I've overstepped healthy boundaries, and I've tried to clean up the garbage. I've got a husband who loves me just the way I am (although I could be a few pounds lighter) and my friends are accepting. So why was I having such a hard time writing these chapters on forgiveness?

Then about half way through the first book, I began to feel conviction. I was not as guiltless as I had assumed. I had caused hurt, although unintentionally—and I had been hurt. Two very good reasons to seek and extend forgiveness. And now the struggle began. Should I; should I not? And I asked every one of those questions that I posed in the preceding pages of this chapter.

My first reflection was of my own hurt and my need to extend forgiveness to the person who had been responsible for my mother's death and the severe dislocation of my foot (it had literally been knocked off my leg bone) leaving me with pain at every step. I never really blamed her. It was an accident. She was a young mother who made one momentary mistake; she looked back to check to see if her five-year-old daughter was seat-belted in, strayed over the center line into my lane, and we met going full speed at the top of the hill. I called twice immediately after the accident to check on her child who was hurt, but she was never home, and I never thought to tell the relatives I had talked to that I didn't blame her. After Mom died, life took a number of unexpected turns, and it never dawned on me to contact her again. We never sued for damages. Why should we take a young family's home or car away? She should know I wasn't bitter. But did she? Over two years had now gone by. How was she coping? How was her little girl?

Creating Love

I put down the book and walked into my husband's office (we both work at home). Neither of us could remember the mother's name. My husband found the police record of the accident and as I began to read, I came upon her birth date: 1968. I shook my head. Suzanne was the same age as my oldest daughter. Suddenly she became a real person to me. What if this had happened to Kimberly? I would certainly want her to know without a doubt that the victims of her mistake didn't blame her. I thought about writing to Suzanne, but I was consumed with an urgent desire to contact her. I found her name in the phone book, called, woke her up (I didn't know she worked the third shift and slept early evening hours), and said those bottled-up words, "I know it was an accident. I don't want you to feel guilty. I never blamed you." As evidence of my sincerity, I told her to drop by my house. and I'd give her a book I had written about working mothers, since she was one. But when I hung up, I thought, *she'll never do it*. It would take a lot of guts to go to the house of a stranger whose mother died because of her mistake. So I packed up the book and some children's tapes of *Kim, Kari, and Kevin Stories* and sent them to her with a note saying that I didn't blame her. I wanted her to have the words in writing so she could re-read them if she ever doubted.

My heart was a little lighter, but that was the easiest part of the forgiveness work I needed to do. I found it much easier to forgive than to ask forgiveness. I struggled with having to say "I'm sorry" for the next hour. I finally wrote to four people I thought of that I had not meant to hurt. But even though my motives were honorable, my actions had caused them to alienate themselves from me—therefore, telling me that I had hurt them. I had never seen myself as guilty before; it was their fault. They chose to take things wrong. I was only doing my job. I had tried to make friendly contacts with them. They ignored me. *If that's the way they want it,* I had thought, *I could live without associating with them.* I became indifferent. Now I realized, *I was wrong! I was guilty!* The fact that they were hurt was reason enough for me to say, "I'm sorry I caused you hurt."

But to say those words ripped off the robe of my own righteousness! It was the hardest thing I ever had been asked to do—to admit I was wrong.

After the notes were written and posted, I was eager to get back to the book. I was flooded with ideas. I couldn't get it all down. Even now I wonder if I'll be able to convey to you what an incredible experience this thing called forgiveness really is! My own cup is fuller because I've pulled the plug on some stuff I didn't even realize existed because I was too busy to notice and too indifferent to care. I'm sure the Holy Spirit was saying, "There's a lot more, Kay. But I know you can only handle so much at once. You may have tried to do the right things, but your motives weren't always spotless. You've got a lot of pride in your cup, and selfishness. Doubt is there too. It has caused you to make decisions that protected you and inadvertently hurt others. I have even detected an occasional flash of envy. But together, we'll work on it. You've taken the first step."

And my response? "It feels *so* good. I'm ready, Lord, when You are."

Now I challenge you, take some time to reflect on your past. Are there some people in your life who have hurt you physically, psychologically, spiritually, or materially? If you haven't yet extended the olive branch of forgiveness, isn't it time? If you've forgiven them in your heart, shouldn't you let them know and free them from the burden of guilt?

And are there people you've hurt: a child, a spouse, a

friend, a neighbor, a co-worker, a fellow believer? If you feel the tug of the Holy Spirit on your heart, don't delay. Forgiveness is a wonderful gift for both the giver and the receiver. Flush away the negative dregs in your cup with miracle-working forgiveness and experience the grace of God filling your love cup.

Chapter Ten

Steps to Forgiveness

"A wise man will make haste to forgive,
because he knows the full value of time
and will not suffer it to pass away
in unnecessary pain."
—*Rambler*

There should never be a doubt about whether or not to forgive someone who has wronged you. Forgiveness should not be conditional upon repentance. Complete forgiveness involves two people, the offender and the offended, but the process of forgiveness may start with either. Most often as a parent or a mature adult, forgiveness must start with you.

At all times forgiveness should be given freely, reconciliation sought, and the incident "forgotten." But sometimes forgiveness is a pretense. False forgiveness is pretending you are forgiving when you're really not—it's a way of sabotaging the process. Instead of filling a love cup, false forgiveness empties it. There is a lot of false forgiveness being practiced among families and friends. It's a way of undermining loving relationships.

There are five steps to complete forgiveness. Step 1: Recognizing the problem. Step 2: Accepting personal responsibility for your behavior. Step 3: Having a repentant and forgiving attitude. Step 4: Working toward reconciliation. Step 5: Forgetting or choosing not to recall. At each step there may be a temptation to halt or damage the forgiveness process.

Step 1: Recognize the problem

When is forgiveness necessary? Life is filled with bumps and bruises. Does every minor scrape require that one go through the five steps of forgiveness? No. It's only when we feel or cause relationship-breaking hurt that forgiveness is essential. It's only when we catch ourselves having thoughts of ill-will for the other that the forgiveness process needs to be initiated.

The first way you can falsify forgiveness is to think that you're guiltless, so you never initiate the process. But you can also err on the other extreme by becoming paranoid, and at every mistake, you make it into a federal case by seeking unnecessary forgiveness. If people hurt you unintentionally, you don't need to confront them and make them feel bad because your sensitive nature has accused them of wrongfully hurting you. A better way to handle this would be to say, "Lord, I'm far too sensitive, and I got my feelings rubbed the wrong way. Forgive me for letting little things cause me to doubt my personal value as Your child, a descendant of royalty—the King of the Universe. Fill me up with Your love and help me to not take myself so seriously."

When there is a breaking of a relationship—when you feel an estrangement—that's where forgiveness needs to kick in, whether you "feel" guilty or not.

If you deny there's a problem, it's futile to start the forgiveness process. It's halted prematurely; love can't shine through because reconciliation cannot take place. If you deny the problem, you sabotage the first step.

The deny-er is a person who, when confronted with a mistake or injustice, or asked to forgive it, denies any knowledge of the problem. "Who me? What problem? There's nothing wrong. You're just imagining the whole thing!"

Sometimes someone asks forgiveness for a minor matter. The person thought he or she had hurt you, but to you the incident was of no significance. What should you do? The tendency is to deny: to say, "It was nothing." But by denying, you withhold forgiveness. In a way you are telling the person who asks for forgiveness that he or she was wrong to be so sensitive. This makes the person feel worse. It would be better to simply say, "Forgiven."

A number of years ago I was complaining to a professional friend of mine about someone who was acting obnoxious, persecuting me with picky complaints, and making false assumptions about the motives behind my behavior. You should ask forgiveness, was the advice I got. "Wait a minute," I said, "I haven't done anything wrong. What do I have to ask forgiveness for?"

He proceeded to say, "Well, you haven't been all that accepting of her, have you?"

"Well???"

"Well, maybe you ought to apologize."

I didn't like the advice I got. My professional friend was all too perceptive. I knew he was right. I had been quite open about my lack of acceptance! But since I did want to break this stalemate, I decided to follow his advice.

I waited until there was a time when we were alone, swallowed hard, and said, "I want to let you know I'm sorry for not being very accepting of you. And I'd like you to forgive me for my negative attitude."

And the response? A slap in the face. Not a literal one. And surely not an intentional one. The person, merely said, "I don't know what you're talking about." A total denial of the problem. The words, "You're forgiven," would have been so sweet, and so affirming to justify the incredible amount of courage I had to muster up to admit my fault. Now I was doubly accused. Not only did this person question my motives, which was the problem in the first place, but now she questioned my perception of the problem alienating us. But regardless of the seeming failure of my bumbling attempt at initiating the forgiveness process, from then on a more accepting and open relationship developed between us.

So, even if you just get to the first or second step of the forgiveness process—it can have an impact for good. Don't get discouraged!

Step 2: Accept personal responsibility

Recognize that you were at fault—at least in part. You can't ask forgiveness if you can't recognize your own error. Accusers sabotage this step. They blame others for their own mistakes.

One day, four-year-old Kevin was helping plant roses. We had just dug three giant holes and filled them with water. The phone rang, I ran to answer it, leaving Kevin to guard the holes. The temptation was too much. By the time I returned, Kevin was knee-deep in water, shoes and all.

Kevin heard me coming. Too late, he figured that shoes and muddy water were a poor combination. Before I fully realized what had happened, he shouted, "Someone pushed me in!"

No one was there. Just Kevin. He knew that; so did I. I muttered, "Oh, someone pushed you in," and returned to the roses, waiting to see what Kevin would do next. He splashed and stomped, perhaps waiting for my reprimand. My calm acceptance of what he knew had to be unacceptable behavior, puzzled him. Soon he asked, "Mommy, when you were a little girl, did your mother let you splash in muddy water with your shoes on?"

Kevin had no reason to blame someone else. I hadn't reacted negatively by threatening or criticizing. But he wasn't taking a chance. Almost by reflex, when he misbehaved, his first reaction was to blame someone else.

The tendency to blame another is so human. It's almost like the original sin. Satan blamed God for rules he couldn't keep. Adam blamed Eve . . . and on and on, down through the generations to Kevin blaming a "someone" who didn't exist.

Blaming someone else goes beyond childhood. Picture yourself in these common situations:

Company comes. You're behind schedule; things are in a mess. You turn to the family: "If you had gotten up on time and helped me like you should, this wouldn't have happened."

You receive a speeding ticket. Angrily, you turn to the kids in the back seat, "Why didn't you get ready quicker? I wouldn't have had to drive so fast!"

You trip over some paint cans you had left in the garage. Your teenager gets the blame: "You've been home all day, why didn't you pick up these cans?"

Blaming others is promoted by a punitive atmosphere where wrongs are not forgiven. Some people will go so far as to lie, cheat, or accuse others in order not to get caught.

Failure to accept responsibility for your own acts is a harmful habit. It promotes irresponsibility and a self-righteous, holier-than-thou attitude.

It is psychologically damaging to live with an accuser because accusers blame everyone, including the innocent. Once the accusation is cast, doubts are planted in the minds of others. Who should others believe, you or your accuser? Your character is questioned. And it takes character to keep yourself from repaying evil with evil.

Don't let people succeed in blaming others; don't tolerate it in yourself. Let others know that it's all right to be wrong. Everyone makes mistakes. That's how we learn. Be quick to admit your own mistakes; don't indulge in blaming others, even though you might have a case. Let your children model your words, "I should have known better." "I goofed." Next time I'll ask first." "I shouldn't have gotten angry."

It's the big person who can own up to his or her mistakes. Such a person commands respect. And you'll respect yourself more when you, too, are willing to take personal responsibility.

Step 3: Have a repentant, forgiving attitude

"I'm sorry," are magic words. At least parents often think they are. How often do parents seek them from a child? But does "I'm sorry" really mean repentance? Hardly. True repentance is an attitude more than a behavior. Saying, "I'm sorry" is not enough unless we carry through with a genuine "sorry" attitude.

We all know false repenters. They say the magic words, "I'm sorry," often through clenched teeth and with fisted hands. Together with "I'm sorry" come the barbs—often sub-verbal—"I'll get you next time!" or "I'll never forget what you did to me!"

To force repentance leads to dishonesty. An irate dad threatened his son who had just trampled through the garden to catch a fly ball: "Say I'm sorry!"

"How can I?" implored the boy, "I'm not sorry, and you told me not to lie."

Forcing repentance is a sabotage of the process. "I'm sorry" becomes a ritual devoid of meaning; a magical way to set things straight. A way to avoid the steps toward reconciliation.

Don't push people to say "I'm sorry" when they aren't. Wait until tempers have cooled. A repentant spirit is impossible when anger and revenge dominate. When they subside, you can return to the issue, talk about the need to put things right, and discuss solutions. For some, this cooling off period may take days. Always make it easy for the erring. Leave the door to repentance open. If you are too pushy, the natural tendency for the other is to resist.

It is much easier for the innocent to offer forgiveness than for the offender to ask. Even accepting forgiveness is tough because it admits guilt. When you have offended someone and they initiate the forgiveness process by saying, "I forgive you," a simple "thank you," is all that is necessary.

The guilty person often has real difficulty in seeking

forgiveness—it's as if his or her cup is filled to the brim with negative emotions, guilt, hate, bitterness, and revenge—leaving little room for the positive attitudes of repentance or concern for others. Sometimes the best path to repentance is for the one who is least guilty to say "I'm sorry." The response from the other is often, "It wasn't all your fault. I was at fault too." This, then, opens the door for a solution, for getting on with the important business of reconciliation.

Step 4: Working toward reconciliation

Love demands gluing together the broken pieces—reestablishing the relationship. One couple had a "reconciliation rug." They agreed that the first one to step on the rug and start the reconciliation process was the least guilty.

When tempers became heated, they would race to see who would first reach the rug. It was often a tie; they would fall into each others' arms, laugh, and the reconciliation process was under way.

Reconciliation is sabotaged by saying, "I'll forgive you, but don't let it happen again." "You're forgiven, but I won't trust you again." "I forgave him, but now I don't want to have anything to do with him." The Golden Rule is the best guide. Because you enjoy having a full cup, be willing to fill another cup with a full measure of forgiveness.

What if the wrong happened many years ago and it's water under the bridge now? Indifference is an enemy of love. The attitude, "I'm open to reconciliation if the other person wants to make the first move, but at this point I really don't care?" will sabotage the forgiveness process. The model for many hurting relationships is to merely drift apart and become indifferent. Friends are gifts we give ourselves. When friends whom we have invested our time and emotions in drift apart, we lose something precious. Every friendship is worth making an effort to save. Humble yourself, make the contact, even though years old; who knows what time and God's love can restore.

Don't, however, feel forgiveness is a failure if reconciliation cannot be accomplished, because you have no control over the other person. Getting to Step 3 of the forgiveness process is better than nothing at all. It would have been nice to experience a round trip—the cost was the same—but if you can only take a one-way trip, all is not lost. You can still move on to step 5.

Step 5: "Forgetting" or choosing not to recall

I hate to be reminded of past mistakes. I was once worried that a traffic ticket would mar my previously spotless record. "Don't worry," I was told, "in three years the state of California deletes the violation." That made me feel better. In three years it would be gone. The record shredded.

Remembering past mistakes clouds your expectations of that person. A record of misbehavior makes you expect more of the same. Children tend to live out parental expectations. It can be a vicious circle.

But is it really possible to forget? In reality our minds are like computers that automatically save everything. Every sensation, every stimuli that enters our consciousness is stored someplace in the marvelous brain cell network of neurons and connectors that make up the intelligence center of our bodies.

Unless a lobotomy is performed or in some other way the memory portion of your brain is destroyed, it's impossible to erase events from your mind. But you can choose consciously to ignore them and certainly not to talk about them. When a memory flashes into your consciousness, you can choose to think of something pleasant. You can pray a blessing on the one who hurt you. The old thought patterns are never lost, but the continual use of the new ones—replacing good memories for bad—is like forging a new path through the forest. Eventually, the old grows over, and the new dominates. But it won't happen by chance. It takes determined effort to retrain your thinking: to forgive so completely that you "forget."

The good news is that the Creator of our computer system has a way of erasing! When those mistakes—those painful memories—are buried as deep as the deepest sea. They're gone!

Henry Ward Beecher once said, " 'I can forgive, but I cannot forget,' is only another way of saying, 'I will not forgive.' Forgiveness ought to be like a canceled note, torn in two and burned up so that it never can be shown against one."

How do you know you have been successful in this process of "forgetting"? When you can focus on the future with no regrets for the past.

Have you ever noticed how easily children forget we have occasionally wronged them or caused them pain? I was watching two young children playing together at the beach. Some misunderstanding must have occurred for suddenly I heard them screaming, "That's not fair. I hate you. I'll never play with you again." Some pretty bitter words. I dozed and then a few minutes later looked over at the war zone. The bitter enemies were gone. Instead, I saw two happy children playing together. I've often wondered if that's why Jesus said we must become like little children in order to enter heaven, willing to quickly forgive and forget.

Let's forgive. Let's recognize the problem, accept personal responsibility, show a repentant or forgiving attitude, be willing to start the reconciliation process, and choose not to recall—to forget. Forgiveness makes it possible to replace the hurt, bitterness, injustice, and prejudice with positive feelings of love. It can change empty lives into full ones.

Chapter Eleven

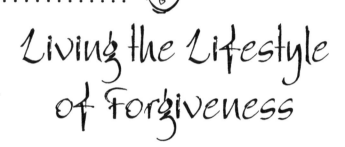

Living the Lifestyle of Forgiveness

"Love forgets mistakes;
nagging about them parts the best of friends."
—*Proverbs 17:9, The Living Bible*

It was a small thing. "Sweetheart, I put a tape in the VCR to catch that three-hour special on teen violence you wanted to see."

"Hey, thanks. Were you able to find a blank tape?"

"Well, not exactly. I'm taping over Clinton's inaugura-tion."

"You did find the *Heart for Olivia* tape, didn't you?

"I never saw it."

"You had to. I told you I left it in the VCR, but hadn't written the title on it."

"You never told me."

"I did too. I told you I taped it for the kids to watch."

"I don't know where it is."

"What do you mean, you don't know? You took it out of the VCR!"

"I don't remember taking it out!"

"I can't believe this is happening! It was right there."

"It's not my fault. You should have labeled it."

"Don't blame me. You took it out of the VCR."

By now you're probably catching the gist of the "conversation." How would you finish it?

It depends on the lifestyle you're living. If you merely do what comes naturally, you'll "end" the silly argument with someone getting hurt. The natural lifestyle is emotionally-based, impulsive action that demands justice. Tempers skyrocket, things are thrown. Maybe not the video tape or the VCR. More likely a laundry load of "play-dirty" slams and accusations!

Once hurt is felt, there must be forgiveness before you can get back on the road to reconciliation. The natural lifestyle leads down the rocky trail of tears. When the trek gets tough, when couples find a Mt. Everest or the Grand Canyon in their path, they opt out. Rather than rubbing each other's hurts with the salve of forgiveness, they lick their own wounds and limp to the divorce courts. Simply put, the natural lifestyle is to out-think, out-talk, and out-wit your partner until someone's in the out-house!

The forgiveness lifestyle is completely different. Those living continually with the spirit of forgiveness in their hearts don't allow anger and resentment to build. Their main desire is reconciliation, not punishment. They are quick to forgive and forget. Instead of erring on the side of justice, they would risk erring on the side of mercy. They might end this "conversation" with:

Humor. "I bet if this were being videotaped, we'd win America's Most Ridiculous Home Video Argument!" Humor is a great road paver to forgiveness.

Reality. "I can't believe I'm so upset about that *Heart for Olivia* video, when what I should be saying is I really appreciate your taping that special I wanted to watch!" When you take time to point out the reality of the situation, it gives both sides an opportunity to reassess the validity of their positions.

Time-out "I don't really like the direction we're heading. Before we say anything else, let's go in and see if we can't find that video." When you need a winning strategy, time-out is a great way to help you refocus.

Diversion. "If we're not careful we're both going to have a heart attack over that *Heart for Olivia* tape. And talking about heart attacks—maybe what we both need right now is a good jog around the block." Sometimes arguments aren't worth taking time to solve. Diverting your attention to something fun or meaningful that you can do together will help you reevaluate whether or not the argument needs to be revisited.

Apologies. "I don't know what got into me. I'm sorry I'm acting like this." When "I'm sorry" comes early before the hurt has time to sink in, it's fairly painless to offer and easily accepted!

Word Pictures. "I feel like we've just fallen out of our boat and are caught in the current of a river flowing toward Niagara Falls. The longer we drift away from the safety of the boat the stronger the current becomes. I'm ready to throw you a life preserver and climb back in our boat. What about you?"

Reaffirmation of Love. "Honey, I love you, and that's the most important thing." It's amazing how quickly a reaffirming hug and kiss can clear up blurred thinking.

The lifestyle of forgiveness motto is Ephesians 4:26. It has two fundamental safety nets to protect family members from hurting each other:

1. *"Be angry, and do not sin."* You can't control the onset of emotion. Don't kid yourself. You will get angry. But living the lifestyle of forgiveness, you won't harbor anger, express negative emotions in hurtful ways, or demand punishment.

2. *"Do not let the sun go down on your wrath."* And if by chance anger slips past the first safety net and turns to wrath, causing hurt and misunderstanding, it will never be for more than 24 hours. The forgiveness lifestyle demands restitution before the sun goes down!

The paradigm shift

How can one live the lifestyle of forgiveness? It all has to do with the way you see your world. Everyone has a different perception of reality—a different model from which decisions are made—a different paradigm.

Children are born egocentric. In other words, they are self-centered. They view the world as revolving around themselves. If they are holding something, it is theirs. They are the cause of events around them. If they think something, it's true. Others are merely an extension of themselves to manipulate and control. This is a self-preservation modality.

Creating Love

Growing up means to move from self-centeredness to other-centeredness. A paradigm shift. Some are more successful than others in achieving this goal. It means seeing others as individuals with their own ideas, values, personalities, talents, and perceptions. It means realizing that others have the same rights of personhood as yourself.

If a child's personhood is physically or psychologically threatened, the natural instinct is to stay in a self-preservation modality, closing one's eyes to the possibility that there are two ways (or an infinite number of ways) to view reality. Because of experiences of childhood, many people grow up physically and marry, without being able to grow out of their childhood egocentric pattern of thinking.

Seeing things from another's point of view is risky, because you don't control all the options. But it is absolutely essential if one is to live the forgiveness lifestyle.

Without forgiveness seemingly minor parent/child conflicts with the resultant negative feelings get bagged and never dumped. The child ends up with a lot of leftover garbage that can get in the way of other relationships. Getting married with unresolved parent/child issues is risky. If these issues don't crop up and interfere with your marriage relationship, they are sure to affect your relationship with your own children. It's much better to dispose of the garbage bags as soon as possible, rather than stumble over them for the rest of your life!

But forgiveness to be complete isn't a one-way trip. It requires a paradigm shift by both offended parties. The younger the child, the more difficult it is because of the child's egocentric nature. That's why consequences that get the point across that parents mean what they say and say what they mean are sometimes painful. The safer the child's environment, however, the more trusting the relationship (see the next chapter), the sooner the child will be able and open enough to see things from the parent's point of view. On the other hand; the more parents push, the more unsafe the child feels, and the more difficult it will be for the child (regardless of age) to experience a paradigm shift.

In parent/child relationships it is the parent who must be responsible for approaching problems in such a way that the child will be most open to understanding the parent's point of view. In a healthy parent/child relationship this responsibility shifts as the child matures and remains fairly balanced in healthy parent/adult child relationships. As the parent advances into old age, there might be a shift where the adult child will now take more responsibility.

But in marriage the responsibility for approaching problems in such a way that each person is open to the other's point of view should be 50/50! Obviously a perfect balance is unlikely. But never should it be only one person's responsibility. The more one-sided the marriage, the more it begins to resemble a parent/child relationship. Just as the natural outcome of a parent/child relationship is independence, so it is in marriage. When there is imbalance, the chances are great that one or the other will opt out of the relationship.

The question is, how do you go about approaching problems in such a way that each is open to the other's point of view?

1. Keep calm. Emotion muddies clear thinking and skews perception.

2. Acknowledge the fact that the other person has a different point of view.

3. Allow the other person to clarify his or her point of view.

4. Ask for permission to clarify your differing point of view.

5. Ask forgiveness for the hurt you caused the other person.

6. Celebrate your reconciliation. Do something fun together. Break your diet and share a dish of ice cream. Hug. Celebration of reconciliation is important because we tend to do only those things that we are rewarded for doing. The process of forgiveness is painful; it's tough to admit that you hurt someone; it's humbling to confess a mistake. But if the reconciliation after the confession is pleasant enough, it can give you the motivation you need to get over the pain as quickly as possible and revel in the reward.

Media models of forgiveness

One of the reasons a lifestyle of forgiveness is so difficult to live is because our world is greatly lacking in appropriate models. Take the media model, for example:

Scene 1. Hurtful words and foul name calling appears to be an acceptable way of talking to each other. Words so bad they have to be cut or "bleeped" out before a program can be shown on television come spewing out of the good guys as well as the bad. The most damaging is the "family" sitcoms where there is a constant barrage of name-calling and put-downs, as if this is the way families should live. And seldom, if ever, is there any indication that these words hurt another person. Never does someone say, "I'm sorry" for calling another the back end of a donkey! (I can't even bring myself to write the word, let alone say it out loud.) And taking the Lord's name in vain is just as common. Total disrespect for our Creator leads to total disrespect for the created. People are treated as objects—not people!

Granted, values differ, but if there is no respect for the personhood and feelings of another, the need for forgiveness is nullified. Instead, relationships are discarded like cheap, used paper plates, and we merely find another supply. Too many families today accept the language of media as household language, destroying word by word the personhood of each other.

Scene 2. The sensitive, forgiving person is ridiculed as weak, soft, and terribly misguided. "Get real," is the message we are given. "You've got to fight for your rights. As long as you're stronger, it doesn't matter what other's think. Besides, if we fight and I apologize first, it will look like I was in the wrong. And to be wrong is to be weak." The whole gang scene portrays this vividly. Goldie Bristol, author of *When It's Hard to Forgive*, explains, "Anytime we forgive, whether the offense is petty or serious, we are consenting to be wronged. We give up our rights and that is always costly. It hurts. We agree to bear the pain of the other person's wrong action." And so the violence escalates. None is willing to admit wrongdoing. Instead, the passion is revenge; to get even. And the result is that families are trapped in the "killing fields of America" because they are willing to believe a media lie—that the forgiving person is weak. Yet in reality the opposite is true. All who have experienced it can testify that it takes an incredible amount of strength to admit you're wrong and ask for forgiveness.

Scene 3. Relationships are portrayed as contracts, not commitments. A contract is only good if you're getting something out of it; something for something. As soon as the relationship is no longer giving the person something meaningful, the contract is broken, and the person wants out. Soaps are full of this. People slip in and out of bed with each other, not because of commitment but because they want fulfilled passion or something else. And when the affair is over, they grow indifferent and move on. If relationships are contracts, there is no need for forgiveness. Just move on to another contract. The result, which is seldom clearly portrayed, is an incredible sense of loneliness, alienation, and psychological pain.

Friendship, to develop, requires an investment of time. And with time comes self-disclosure, with self-disclosure comes intimacy, and with intimacy—bonding. When there is physical involvement, the psychological bond becomes stronger. Sexual intercourse is given by God to only one type of relationship, marriage. It is God's symbol of commitment to a lifelong, one-flesh relationship. At any stage of bonding in a friendship, should breakup occur, there is pain. That's the nature of bonding. The more bonded, the more a person will suffer when there's a breakup. That's why divorce is so devastating. To move in and out of bonding relationships is painful. Media portray mere indifference. Sometimes it may appear so in real life, but the appearance of indifference is only a defense mechanism to mask the incredible hurt on the inside. Contracts are for objects. Commitments are for people.

Forgiving your parent

At the end of a presentation on the love-cup principle a woman who looked to be about retirement age came up to me and lamented, "You have no idea how hard it is to find a Mother's Day card or a birthday card for my mother that doesn't have the word 'love' in it. I've spent all my life looking. I have never loved my mother. She's in a nursing home now. I wish I could love her, but I'm afraid it's impossible."

I listened to a story about a mother whose own love cup was empty. She constantly was yelling at this girl who, in her mother's eyes, could do nothing right. And even though the girl dearly loved her father, the mother appeared jealous and did everything possible to keep the girl away from him.

One specific incident this woman related was when, as a little girl, she would get in the cab of their pickup truck and would attempt to sit in the middle by her dad, her mother would say, "That's my place," and roughly yank her up and put her by the window.

I made the comment, "Maybe you need to ask your mom for forgiveness and tell her you forgive her."

"What do you mean?" she exclaimed. "I didn't do anything wrong. She's the one who needs to ask forgiveness!"

I mentioned her mother probably had no idea that she inflicted psychological pain on her daughter. And it would be cruel to bring specific things up that chances are her mom wouldn't remember. It would only hurt her feelings. Instead, let forgiveness be offered in sacrificial love. Say, "Mom, we both made mistakes when I was a child. I want you to know that I forgive you for the things you did that hurt me, and I want you to forgive me for holding these things against you all these years. I'd like to wipe the slate clean." And then say those three magic words, "I love you."

She did it, and told me later she has an entirely new relationship with her mother. Forgiveness was the key that unlocked her heart to love.

Some counseling professionals say to heal a painful past, you have to confront a parent with the exact sins they committed. I agree you've got to get your painful memories out, but to confront the person who has caused the pain is not always appropriate. There is never a time when anyone should willfully hurt another; not even in an attempt to heal yourself. There are other ways to absolve the hurt. For example, God has broad shoulders and can take your bag of garbage without it having to hurt others.

I've seen older parents totally devastated when their children have accused them of things they had no idea they had done. Or perhaps the parents had done these things with a healthy motive, but they were misinterpreted by the child. Harsh behavior may be abusive to one child, and seen by another as fair discipline. Parents may have thought they were being good parents, but because of the child's personality makeup, their "good" behavior was painful. So one must be careful when blame is cast in these gray areas. The wrong might not be necessarily what the person did, but that the person was not perceptive enough to realize what it was doing to you.

If the "sin" is an open one, and there is no doubt that both child and parent are aware it happened, then open confrontation may be appropriate. I say "may be" because victims should not put themselves in a situation where they are made to feel guilty once again. This can happen, especially in a confrontation concerning sexual abuse. A counselor can help you make the decision and coach you on how to handle the forgiveness issue.

Perhaps the safest thing to do, when trying to get rid of the bags of garbage from your childhood, is to apply the Golden Rule: treat your parents as you would like to be treated by your children.

Forgiving yourself

Perhaps the hardest person in the world to forgive is yourself. Everyone makes mistakes, but the magnitude of the error, even if known only to you, can heap a pile of guilt. Parents are good at blaming themselves when their children don't turn out the way they had hoped. For example, here's a letter I once received:

> Dear Dr. Kuzma: Please cancel my subscription to the *Family Times* newspaper. Our son is out of the nest and we flubbed up so much when we did have him that your newsletter renews my guilt trip each time I receive it. Our eighteen-year-old is a rebel. He is on his own and we have broken hearts over his wasted life. The newspaper is too late for our household. It is very good and wise counsel for the parents of younger children. I just hope and pray these couples will take heed. Signed: "A sad but wiser mother."

Most parents have at times said, "If only we could have a second chance." "If only" are probably the saddest two words that have ever been spoken. But "If only" will never right the wrongs. It just keeps sensitive parents heaped to overflowing with guilt.

If you are feeling guilty about the mistakes you have made parenting your children, you must forgive yourself. There is no such thing as a perfect parent. Chances are you did the best you knew how to do. If you didn't plan to maliciously hurt your child, it's irrational to feel guilty. You simply didn't know any better. Your children have the power to choose whether or not they will allow the mistakes you made to ruin their lives. Don't allow them to blame their current mistakes on your past behavior.

If guilt persists (and chances are it will), you have got to do something about it. My suggestion is to simply say, "I'm sorry." Once you have asked for forgiveness, it's up to your child to choose whether or not he will accept your apology.

Then, turn your thoughts to the positive. Remember, it's never too late to start filling your child's love cup. Compliment him, wink or smile at him, do kind things for him. Your show of affection must not be dependent on his behavior. You can act respectful towards him, even when you can't approve of his behavior.

When Russ went to Vietnam, he got mixed up with all kinds of behavior that his parents disapproved of: drugs, sex, tobacco. His parents were obviously disappointed when he came home a chain smoker. Russ knew how offensive smoking was to his dad, and the first time he stepped into the home with a cigarette in his hand he expected to be kicked out. Instead, his dad put an arm around him and said, "Russ, you know how I dislike smoking, but if that's the only way I can have you home, I guess I'll just have to get used to it, 'cause you're more important to me than the smoking."

Russ was so shocked with his dad's response that he never again smoked in his presence. He respected his dad too much. The end of the story is a happy one. Russ eventually gave up those negative behaviors and became a pastor.

Of course, that's just one example, and for every positive one, there are probably a dozen negative ones. Regardless of the statistics, however, the winning principle remains the same: forgiveness heals separation and guilt, while bitterness only makes it fester.

Finally, take hold of that marvelous promise in Isaiah 49:25, where God says that He will contend with those that contend with us, and He will save our children.

Forgiving yourself for the death of a child

Death is a part of life. But somehow it's much easier to accept when it comes in old age than when it strikes down a child, especially when you feel you were somehow responsible!

A father, I'll call him Steve, was driving late one night on a long, lonely strip of highway and fell asleep at the wheel. You can guess the rest. The van rolled, trapping the family inside. Badly hurt, he and his wife found their baby girl hurt, but alive. But their little boy was thrown out of the van and by the time they found him he was hardly breathing. They managed to get him to the roadside, but the highway was deserted. An hour passed before someone stopped and by that time it was too late.

When I heard the story, Steve and his wife were both in Salvation Army training. Smiles lit up their faces, and they radiated a sense of hope.

I knew there were so many other families who were hurting with a similar loss. What could this family tell me that might be of help to others? I boldly asked, "You must have felt guilty about the accident. How were you able to handle it?"

"Yes," Steve said, "I know I'm to blame, because if I hadn't fallen asleep, it wouldn't have happened. But it was an accident. I didn't mean to fall asleep, so it's important I don't condemn myself. I'll always have to live with the consequence of not having my boy, but I believe that I have a responsibility to look for the benefits in every situation, including this one. For example, my wife and I are just completing our Salvation Army training. I don't know if we'd have done this if it weren't for the accident. We want to make something of our lives and help others. I want to be a better person—not bitter."

Without self-forgiveness, you'll end up carrying a bag of guilt, anger, and bitterness through the rest of your life, and stumble over it in your other relationships. When tragedy happens to families, either it draws them closer together as they rely on each other for strength and hope. Or they split. Over half do! And the reason is because they are stumbling over the garbage of unresolved negative emotion. If you find yourself struggling with guilt, seek professional help. God has forgiven you. Forgive yourself. Living the lifestyle of forgiveness means extending it to yourself.

Forgiving God

When bad things happen, we sometimes blame God. God doesn't need our forgiveness because He never makes mistakes, but because we don't have a God-perspective on life, it's easy for us to judge. Forgiving God is important for our own happiness and well-being.

In reality every act of God must be seen through the "great controversy" that is currently raging between good and evil; between Christ and Satan. Satan is trying in every possible way to tarnish God's reputation and have people point the finger of blame at God.

God has the power to break sin now, to destroy evil, to take away all hurt and pain, but sin has not yet run its full course. When the universe fully sees the true nature of sin, then God can say, "Enough. It is finished."

Prayer gives God permission to break into Satan's territory (this world) and work miracles of love and healing. Jesus Himself said that if we had faith even as small as a mustard seed we could move mountains with God's power. But obviously we are lacking. And since so many bad things happen in our world that we don't understand, it's easy to blame God.

What we need is a paradigm shift. We need God's perspective. With understanding, we won't need to blame and harbor bitterness. When I was struggling with the question of "Why did it happen, God?" a friend told me the following parable. Although I have no idea who first told this story I share it hoping that if you're blaming God for the bad things that happen to you, you'll begin to see that God's ways are not necessarily our ways.

Once upon a time a Man of God and a traveler took a journey together. About sundown the first day the Man of God led the traveler to a modest home and knocked on the door. A kind man invited them in and treated them like royalty. After a very pleasant evening together the host showed them a goblet made of pure gold. "This cup means very much to me because my neighbor, who has been an enemy, gave it to me as a token of friendship."

The next morning the Man of God and the traveler thanked their host and started on their way. They had only walked a short distance when the Man of God said, "Wait here. I forgot something." He went back to the house and secretly entered the door. When he returned he had the beautiful gold goblet.

The traveler was shocked. Why had the Man of God taken it?

That night the two stopped at a large landowner's mansion. "Bam, bam, bam," went the large brass knocker. Finally, the door swung open, and a tall inebriated man shouted, "Yeah, wadda you want?"

When the tyrannical landowner heard their request for lodging, he grunted, "Wadda ya think I run here, a hotel?" As they turned to leave, he yelled, "You can sleep in the barn if you want."

In the middle of the night the landowner crept to the pack that belonged to the Man of God, searched it, and quietly removed the goblet. The traveler wanted to stop the thief, but the Man of God whispered, "Wait. All will be well." Again the traveler was confused by the strange behavior of the Man of God.

The next night they found themselves in a dense forest known to be the home of a band of robbers. They knocked at the door of a small cabin. The father hesitated when the men asked for lodging, but his boy insisted they should stay.

After supper the boy settled himself at the foot of the Man of God and listened attentively to the stories he told. He seemed drawn to the Man of God and in the morning asked his father if he could go with them to the fork in the road and show them the way. As they crossed the narrow bridge the boy slipped and fell into the raging river. The traveler plunged into the icy water to save the lad, but it was too late. And all this time the Man of God did nothing.

This was too much for the traveler. In agony he shouted to the Man of God, "What kind of a person are you anyway? You steal from the kind man, allow a tyrant to steal from you, and then just stand by while a boy drowns! Why? Tell me why!"

At last the Man of God said, "It is not for most travelers to understand the ways of God, but for a moment I will open your eyes. The cup the enemy had given to the kind man was poisoned, and I wanted no harm to come to him. I allowed the landowner to steal the goblet because he may choose to drink from it, and the peasants will be free from his rule. And the boy," tears came to his eyes, "the boy loved me. But his father was the head of a gang of robbers, and if the boy had lived, he, because of his love for his father, would have followed in his father's steps. I allowed him to die to save him for eternity."

The traveler at last nodded his head, "I understand," he said.

Chapter Twelve

Being Trustworthy

"To be trusted is a greater compliment
than to be loved."
—*James Ramsay MacDonald*

Elsa Einstein, the wife of the intellectual giant that gave the world the theory of relativity, was once asked if she understood it. "No," she replied, "I don't understand my husband's theory of relativity, but I know my husband, and I know he can be trusted." There is no greater compliment that Elsa could have given her husband.

Trust is the foundation for love. Trust is glue for lasting relationships. Trust is the stuff out of which emerges a psychologically healthy human being.

A child's early environment sets the stage for either dysfunction and relational pain, or for healthy attitudes and behaviors that culminate in meaningful, lasting relationships. And trust is at its core. The window of opportunity is narrow. The most critical year, the first. If children do not learn in the first twelve months of life that their world is a trustworthy place; that the significant people they live with can be trusted to meet their needs; that regardless of what they do, they can trust that they'll be treated with care, respect, acceptance, and forgiveness, they will be denied optimal psychological growth.

Trust is like water to a fish. It gives individuals the freedom to be, to grow, to explore, to create, to test. It surrounds growing children with the security they need to find out about their world. To live is to risk. Trust takes much of the risk out of life, freeing psychological energy from the survival modality, to be expended in growth opportunities and the building of relationships.

As children grow, many families fail their children by not knowing how to maintain a trustworthy environment. During the toddler years, the child asks, "How much of the world is mine to control? Where are my boundaries?" When people fail to establish limits or are inconsistent in their enforcement and allow children too much control, it's frightening to them! Unconsciously children reason, "If I'm the strongest person in my world, who's going to watch out for me?" No longer can children trust others for protection. Security ceases to exist. The defense mechanism is to attempt to control even more. And the dysfunctional connection is made: personal safety becomes attached to control. Children growing up in an insecure environment will through the years become more and more skilled in control techniques: anger, threats, withdrawal, lies, force, violence,

Creating Love

and the list goes on. The result is grownups who constantly test their world to see how much can be controlled. All because of one missing link during the first few years: trust!

But the opposite extreme is equally destructive to healthy psychological growth. That's the environment that is too harsh. It's when children attempt to ask, "How much of the world can I control?" and gets the answer, "Buddy, you're not good enough or capable enough to be trusted to control anything—we're controlling you!" Children never know when they will attempt too much independence or do something outside the boundaries of what the controlling forces in their lives consider appropriate, and they will get their psyche (and sometimes more) "whipped into shape." And the result? Frightened, insecure human beings who retreat into a shell of inferiority and defensiveness. Because they are never allowed to experience the exhilarating feeling of being trusted, they never learn to carry responsibility or be trustworthy.

It's a sad picture, but a picture that is being painted in thousands of children's lives each day. Children who grow up without trust become untrustworthy individuals. Untrustworthy individuals are often highly suspicious. They project their own lack of trustworthiness onto others. They become defensive, self-protective, unwilling to risk, selfish individuals who use and abuse others through control and manipulation, or withdrawal and irresponsibility. And when they have children, the cycle is repeated.

Trust is the key to good psychological health. When children feel trusted, they can risk becoming their own persons. They can bump up against the boundaries and have the security of knowing that if they can handle the added responsibility, their parents will be flexible and allow them the decision; if they can't, the parents will hold firm and make the choice for them. It's a win-win situation. Children win by growing up in a secure, trustworthy environment, and in the process they learn to be trustworthy. Their folks win by having the pleasure of watching self-confident, respectful, and obedient children grow up to be responsible and self-controlled adults. Who could ask for more? And trust is what makes the difference.

Remember the old wives' tale, "Let the baby cry, it's good for the lungs. You don't want the baby to get spoiled!" Well, it's a lie. Research has made it clear that babies who are attended to when they cry are significantly different children at two years of age. They are *not* more spoiled. Instead, because they have established a base of trust in their environment, they can delay gratification without undue upset, while the others are more demanding. It's as if, through the first year of loving attention given to meet a baby's needs, the child is able to say when his mom is detained. "Well, there is no use for me to get too upset. Mom has always come and helped me when I cried before, so I know she'll help me now." Trust is a great security blanket during those early years—and it's one you don't want to give up when you're older!

The key to raising trustworthy children is to model trustworthiness.

The commitment "till death do we part"

In my search for what makes families strong and healthy, I have read dozens of studies, and almost all agree that the most important factor in holding families together in a meaningful relationship is commitment. But things that are worthwhile seldom come easily. And in the heat of a parental argument, children can question their folks' commitment to stay together, "till death do us part."

My husband, Jan, and I discuss all kinds of issues, but rarely argue. We are, however, as vulnerable as everyone else to the stress of time pressures, lack of communication, and misunderstandings, and our tempers can get out of hand, even over insignificant issues. For example, the morning I had told Jan that the kids and I would pick him up during lunch hour so we could get a family picture taken. I had previously mentioned it would be nice to take a family picture by a lake in Riverside, but failed to mention that critical fact on that fateful Tuesday. I didn't get to Jan's office until 12:30. When he got into the car, he casually mentioned that we had better hurry since he had a 1:00 appointment. I blew up. "What?" I exclaimed in an elevated voice. "You can't have a one o'clock! I told you we were going to get our pictures taken?"

"Well, I thought we'd be back by one."

"There's no way. We can't get all the way out to the lake and back in thirty minutes," I wailed.

"Why are we going to the lake?"

"Because I wanted something different."

"Well, let's stop at a phone and tell the photographer to met us here instead."

"I can't!" I yelled, "He's already out at the lake."

"Why didn't you tell me?"

"I did!" Our voices become higher and more staccato.

I don't remember how we resolved the conflict, I just remember that at one point our eight-year-old daughter, Kim, who was sitting quietly in the back seat listening to all of this, spoke up. "I don't want you to ever act like that again!" After that we didn't say much!

Whenever I look at the picture by the lake, with all of us smiling for the camera, I think about the "bumpy" ride that got us there and wonder what is going on behind the smiling faces of those I meet at work, those I sit beside in church, and those I pass at the market or the library.

It's frightening to children when they hear their parents argue, because so many parental arguments "end" in the divorce court. Children question when they hear their folks saying harsh words to each other, "Are you going to get a divorce?" To squelch that fear, you must make it clear that divorce is not an option in your family. I remember Christian author and speaker Josh McDowell saying he made it a point to clarify to his children that he and his wife were committed to stay married for a lifetime and nothing would ever change that. Nothing!

Others have made similar statements. Leo Buscaglia, who has written voluminously on love, said that when his strong, outspoken Italian mother was asked whether she had ever considered divorce, she replied, "Divorce? Never! Murder, often! Divorce never!" (Those married for a number of years can relate to that comment and smile!) The important thing is that regardless of what happens or what a husband and wife might say in the heat of an argument, the children must have the foundation of trust to know without a shadow of a doubt that divorce is not an option.

Annie and Steve Chapman recall the story about Hernando Cortes, the Spanish conqueror of Mexico, and his men burning their ships as a symbol of their commitment to stay in the New World. The Chapmans compare this act to what a couple must do when committing their lives to each other in their song, *The Ships are Burning*. Play it for your children, and let them know you have "burnt the ships" in your lives and are totally committed to the family!

If both bride and groom would truly hold on to that kind of solid commitment to each other, how much more safe and secure their children would feel. The problem today is that divorce *is* an option for many! That fact undermines the foundation of trust. More children now can expect to live in a single-parent home sometime during their growing years than those who will be lucky enough to grow up living with both of their parents.

When I was in graduate school the prevailing feeling was better to divorce than have the children grow up in conflict. The rationale behind that philosophy had to do with trust. Living in conflict without the reassurance that the "ships have been burnt" and their folks have made a commitment to love each other regardless is for a child like living on an earthquake fault. Knowing that the "big" one is expected any day, each small tremor sends terror shooting through their veins. So it is with arguments: each time the child wonders, "Is this the 'big' one?" adrenalin stressors attack the body. Obviously, living on trembling ground is not good for anyone. But is the popular solution of a divorce any better?

Now that researchers have looked at the long-term consequences of divorce, they're changing their minds. Divorce is devastating to a child. *Period.* Even if it is the best solution, it is never a good solution. When divorce puts a permanent chasm between the two most significant people in a child's world, there will be a lifetime of consequences. Every day After Divorce (A.D.) will be significantly different from what the child knew Before Chasm (B.C.). Christmas celebrations will never be the same, nor weekends. Vacations are no longer "family" vacations. The child's perception of family is changed. The child's perception of his or her own identity is changed. Too often mom and dad now become adversaries. In-laws become "outlaws." No longer do all the relatives get together for family reunions. Separation from loved ones is painful, and it occurs on a regular basis. Children are asked to be careful what they say to various significant people, "Don't tell Grandma Jones . . ." Trustworthiness is questioned. Jealousy poisons. Suspicion reigns. Half-truths and sometimes outright lies are told. Children too young to understand issues of the past or too innocent to perceive wounded motives, ask like Pilate did, "What is truth?"

You've seen the fallout. Top of their class, student leader, optimistic kids, suddenly fall behind, drop varsity, quit attending church, become involved with drugs, gangs, or sex, and carry a mountain of insecurities and inadequacies on their shoulders. Others attempt to live above it all and bury their insecurities in achievements, projects, materialism, fanatic religiosity, and a superiority attitude that puts others down in an attempt to lift self. And some withdraw into spending endless hours reading racy novels, watching violent videos, listening to heavy metal, playing addictive Nintendo or Dungeons and Dragons, or exhibiting other escapist behaviors. This is not to say that all children hit the bottom psychologically and act out these self-destructive behaviors when breakup occurs. But none are immune to hurt. And all can benefit from support groups and counseling.

Because divorce is upsetting to children, many feel that it's better if a couple sticks together long enough to get their children raised before they separate and divorce. Perhaps it won't have such a devastating effect? Not necessarily so! Some of the most distressed and wounded kids are those who discover in their late teens that their folks were living a lie all those years. The revelation is like living through an 8.3 quake on the Richter Scale! Suddenly they realize that their foundation of rockbed trust was merely sand. And if they can't trust their folks then who can they trust?

Knowing all this, the best answer to maintaining a foundation of trust for your children is to learn how to communicate, solve problems, and meet each other's needs in constructive ways, and for each to daily renew the marriage commitment to the other with words and acts of love.

Yet, as bad as divorce is, it happens! One can't hold a relationship together alone. And there is no virtue in staying in an abusive one. It only enables the abuser to continue the abuse. Therefore, the question is, how can parents keep their children wrapped in a security blanket of trust when divorce attempts to raise her ugly head?

Give God time to work out Psalm 37 in your life

"Do not fret because of evildoers." If this divorce is not of your choosing, don't be upset, fuss, stew, or brood about what's happening. Verse 3 offers four rules to keep your mind calm through troubled times:

Rule 1. "*Trust in the Lord.*" Just keep trusting that God has your best interests at heart and He is in the process of working things out for you and your children. Read over and over again His words to you in Jeremiah 29:11, "For I know the plans I have for you, says the Lord. They are plans for good and not for evil, to give you a future and a hope" (TLB). And claim the promise God made to the Hebrew parents in Isaiah 49:25 when they were in danger, "I will contend (fight, struggle, wrestle) with him who contends with you, and I will save your children."

Rule 2: "And do good," even if it is the hardest thing in the world to do because of your natural feelings of self-pity, hurt, disappointment, and anger. Think of positive things you can do for others and stir up your emotional energy to do them. It's good therapy to keep yourself busy filling other people's love cups, rather than fretting about something you have no control over.

Rule 3: "Dwell in the land." In other words, dwell calmly in the place where God puts you. If He sees every sparrow that falls, you can be sure He is continually updated on your situation. So don't try to run away from your problems. Until He moves you, stay put! Just don't stubbornly refuse to budge when He opens a door for you.

Rule 4: "Feed on His faithfulness." Think about all the times in the past that God has come through for you. Read Hebrews 11 and energize your faith as you realize what incredible things God has done for His people in the past. Spend time in His Word searching for His promises. Claim them for your own. Meditate on them and write down your thoughts. A year or two from now you'll forget how far God has brought you, unless you take time to record the journey as you're living it.

My favorite verses in Psalm 37 are the following:

> "Delight yourself also in the Lord,
> And He shall give you the desires of your heart.
> Commit your way to the Lord,
> Trust also in Him,
> And He shall bring it to pass" (verses 4, 5).

There is no greater promise in all Scripture. God knows the desires of your heart. Your part is to:

Creating Love

1. *"Delight in Him."* Keep praising God. Joy in the thought of Him. Love Him.

2. *"Commit your way to the Lord."* Literally, "roll your way" to the Lord, as if you're rolling your burden off your shoulders onto His. Give what's happening to you, to Him. Just because the separation and divorce you are going through is your problem in the sense that it can't be blamed on others, it doesn't mean you can't give it to the Lord. But your tendency will be, although you want the Lord to take the psychological burden from your back, to merely ask Him to adjust the straps as you continue to be weighed down with guilt, hurt, and other emotional giants. A good Scripture reference to enhance the meaning of this verse is 1 Peter 5:6, 7, "Therefore, humble yourselves under the mighty hand of God, that He may exalt you in due time, casting all your care upon Him, for He cares for you." It is humbling to not carry your burden by yourself and have to lean on someone else—even God. But if you'll do what He says and merely wait on Him to work things out in His own way within His timetable, you'll experience incredible peace.

3. *"Trust also in Him,"* a re-emphasis of the importance of trust.

There are but two more things you are to do. Read verse 7.

4. *"Rest in the Lord."* To rest here means to be silent. If you will only keep still awhile, rather than filling your life with the noise of jumbled relationships, confused emotions and worldly advice, you will hear in the stillness the voice of God speaking calmness to your soul.

5. *"Wait patiently for Him."* Don't go out and do something foolish or impulsive, trying to work things out for yourself. The counsel is to wait, looking to God for directions, and asking for grace to follow them. Psalm 27:14

elaborates on this phrase,

> Wait on the Lord;
> Be of good courage,
> And He shall strengthen your heart;
> Wait, I say, on the Lord.

This doesn't mean that you should do nothing. But too often the insecurity of living in limbo makes people run ahead of the Lord's timetable. I've seen it happen over and over. Marriage problems lead to separation. Instead of viewing separation as "time-out" to figure out the strategy of how to make the marriage a success, or a time for getting the necessary counseling needed to understand what's been happening in the game of marriage from the other's perspective and then getting back in the game with a winning attitude, couples see separation as the first step toward inevitable divorce!

Rather than trusting their teammate, to whom they committed their life on their wedding day, they begin to distrust and build a brick wall of defense mechanisms to protect themselves. Now the battle lines are drawn. No longer are they playing the marriage game which takes two committed individuals to win. Instead, they are playing the divorce game, which pits two people who have known each other more intimately than anyone else, against each other in a struggle for self-survival, instead of couple-survival. And the tragedy is that not only do the primary players suffer, but everyone on the sidelines suffers too.

The court decree is rendered: *divorced.* Now, instead of waiting on the Lord, there comes an urgent inner need to "move on." Too often this urge is interpreted as moving in an opposite direction—away from your family—and emotional attachments are made to others. Soon another marriage occurs, making reconciliation with the first impossible, or so it seems, and the rift becomes steel.

But if more couples would live out the biblical instruction to "wait on the Lord," it's amazing how things can work out after separation and divorce. Some couples need the symbolism of divorce to bury a destructive marriage and allow God to perform a resurrection. Then with the slate wiped clean, a couple can begin courting and working on their relationship once again. But if one of the partners rushes into another relationship, that handicaps God from working out things to give us the "desires of our hearts." The wisest man who ever lived, and who in his pursuit of happiness married 700 wives and had 300 concubines, spoke from the mouth of experience when he said,

> "And rejoice with the wife of your youth,
> As a loving deer and a graceful doe,
> Let her breasts satisfy you at all times;
> And always be enraptured with her love"
> (Proverbs 5:18, 19).

How long do you wait before moving on to another relationship? Only you and God can determine that. All I know is that among my friends and acquaintances, the majority wish they had waited a little longer. Many have lamented, "Now that I'm in my second marriage, I realize the answer isn't marrying the 'right' person, it's both being committed to making the marriage work. I just wish for my kids' sake I had worked harder on my first marriage. Much heartache and many problems could have been avoided."

Not all second marriages make it. I've known situations where the second marriage—or third—falls apart, and when God has finally been able to make an impact on the person's life, there is a desire to make things right with the first. If there has been a genuine "waiting" on the Lord by the other party, God in His graciousness can put back together what "man" destroyed. But too often, the other has made another commitment that prevents this from happening. And God has to move on to plan 2 for our lives, instead of His original ideal.

If you're struggling with decisions in this area and need help, encouragement, and direction, *Life Partners*, headquarterd in Phoenix, Arizona, offers seminars for healing and a recommitment to lifetime partnership. *Life Skills*, with centers around the country, offer seminars that have proven life-changing and have been successful in saving many marriages. And for those who want a fresh start in a marriage and would like to communicate better, register for a Marriage Encounter weekend. (For more information call Family Matters.)

Chapter Thirteen

Trusting God

"We trust as we love, and where we love . . . .
If we love Christ much,
surely we shall trust Him much."
—*Thomas Brooks*

Do you have an unchanging set of moral standards that guides your life? Living by the philosophy that if it feels good or benefits you, do it, does not promote trust. Children who grow up with the shifting sand of relative morality have difficulty trusting others.

God gave us a sure standard: the Ten Commandments. In summary, we must love God (the first four) and love others (the last six). Specifically, we must make sure that all ten become a way of life. When we do this, we provide our children with an impeccable foundation of trust. You can't argue with something God wrote on stone with His own finger—or something Jesus said that until heaven and earth would pass away that "not even one jot or one tittle" should be changed and that each one was equally important (Matthew 5:17-19).

Turn to Exodus 20 and notice how relevant God's Ten Commandments are for today, and how important each one is in building the foundation of trust within the family.

Commandment 1: "You shall have no other gods before Me." *God wants our trust.* God must come first in our lives. Not money, not material things, not work—not even family. God promises He'll provide all these other things, but first He wants us to trust Him. Trust is the foundation of all relationships—including our relationship to God.

Commandment 2: "You shall not make for yourself any carved image . . . you shall not bow down to them nor serve them." God wants our worship. He wants our loyalty. He wants us! He will accept no substitutes for the real thing. When faced with a choice, God doesn't want us to wallow in confusion. He makes it simple for us; we are to choose a relationship with Him, and Him alone!

Commandment 3: "You shall not take the name of the Lord your God in vain." The Amplified Bible says, "You shall not use or repeat the name of the Lord your God in vain [that is, lightly or frivolously, in false affirmations or profanely]." *God wants our words—our complete allegiance.* He doesn't want us demeaning Him with what we say. Words are incredible influencers, even to ourselves. We tend to believe what we hear. Other people's words influence us. And we tend to believe what we say. Our own words influence us.

Commandment 4: "Remember the Sabbath day, to keep it

holy." God then goes on to clarify which day out of the week He means. "Six days you shall labor and do all your work, but the seventh day is the Sabbath of the Lord your God." God makes it pretty clear, *He wants our time.* God then goes on to specifically instruct us about how we are to keep His day. No one in the household is to work. Then comes His reason for the fourth commandment. God wants one seventh of our time to commemorate the fact that He is the Creator and we are the created. "For in six days the Lord made the heavens and the earth, the sea, and all that is in them, and rested the seventh day. Therefore the Lord blessed the Sabbath day and hallowed it." It's clear God established a memorial in time (something man couldn't lose or manipulate; and something that would continue unchanged through the generations) so we would never forget our significance. We didn't come from monkeys. We weren't born by chance. We were created by the God of the universe! Wow! What incredible feelings of value we should have when we realize this fact. And God wants us to slow down our lives on the seventh day of each week, just as He did at the end of the Creation week, to remember that fact! He doesn't forbid us having celebration days for other important things. The Jews had many holy days—and other rest days they called sabbaths. And we as Christians have done the same with the establishment of a day to celebrate Christ's resurrection. But God's command to remember the seventh day as His special Sabbath with a capital S, still stands, and to deny it is to nullify the significance of the other nine commandments.

Commandment 5: "Honor your father and mother, that your days may be long upon the land which the Lord your God is giving you." After teaching us to honor God with the keeping of the first four commandments, God turns His attention to the next most important relationship of our lives—family. Interestingly, it's the first commandment with a promise. The Kuzma paraphrase is, "If you respect your folks, you can live a good, long life close to home and the family God has given you." Your children's trust in family will be significantly molded by the way you talk about and treat your folks. If they can trust you to honor your own parents, they will be more likely to follow this same model in their relationship with you. If you speak against your folks and act in ways that hurt or demean them, it will cause your children to feel insecure. If you can do this to the people who brought you into the world, burped and fed you and changed your messy pants, there is also the possibility you could treat your own children the same.

Commandment 6: "You shall not murder." Life is sacred. We must never forget that fact.

I think part of the reason there was such an overwhelming outcry demanding the death penalty for Susan Smith, the South Carolina mother who killed her two little boys, was because of the symbolic nature of her hideous act and how it undermines the issue of trust. We might understand, if we stretch our wildest imaginations, the mother who loses control and with temporary insanity batters her child. But no one can understand how a mother could buckle her children into their car seats, drive to the top of a boat ramp, put the car in neutral and get out of the car watching it roll down the ramp and disappear into the lake—and then stand by for forty-five minutes knowing that her precious three-year-old, Michael, and his little brother, Alexander, were struggling for air and dying a slow death by drowning. What must the children's last thoughts of their mother have been?

That act symbolizes the denial of the very trust that holds society together! If we can't trust a mother, who then can we trust?

But, you say, I would never think of killing a person, let alone my own children. Maybe not in the literal sense. But the apostle John calls a spade a spade and says, "whoever hates his brother is a murderer" (1 John 3:15). Jesus expands this commandment to include getting angry without a cause and calling people names, such as "You fool!" (Matthew 5:21-22). Our hate, revenge, bitterness, and anger expressed in words and actions can kill the self-worth of others, and it's our family members who are most at risk. Psychological murder is a slow death. Each careless word and insensitive act wounds. The other way we kill is by failing to fill a person's love cup. We might call that psychological death by starvation!

Instead, our homes should be places where each person is understood and treated with respect. Like Janet Dobrota said when she was a third-grader, "A family means you don't have to pay a five hundred dollar fine for a mistake." Do your kids know that regardless of what happens, their home is a safe place? A letter from Linda, one of my radio listeners, gives a great example of what an ideal home should be:

> We were very discouraged when we moved to this neighborhood six years ago, because all of the children were so cruel and hateful to one another, physically and verbally. Out of fifteen homes, we were the only two-parent family. And there were many problems.
>
> After living here a short time I decided to implement a policy which I shared with each child in the

neighborhood. I told the children that our home and yard would always be a "safe place!" No one playing here would be teased by another, hurt by another, or made fun of. It's a place where we have fun, talk, share, and encourage each other.

The kids depend on me to enforce this policy. Even our carpool to and from school is safe. One time I had to stop the car and let a boy out for foul talk and name calling. He was shocked. A few minutes later, tempers cooled and I let him in. But he never did it again.

Wouldn't it be wonderful if every home—or car—had this "safe-place policy" and enforced it. Children are so tender and can be hurt with unkind words so easily. Sometimes they aren't strong enough to defend themselves. They need a mom or dad to enforce the policy that states: "You may not hurt others." How comforting to know there is a safe place! Every neighborhood needs a refuge like this!

Linda closed her letter with this delightful experience:

The funniest incident occurred about four months ago.

I was sitting in the living room late one afternoon reading to six-year-old Kara and nine-year-old Joshua when I realized there was a lot of commotion in the front yard and on our porch. I opened the door in time to hear one child shouting to the bully in the street, "Go on home and leave us alone. You can't bother us here, 'cuz we're in the Holy yard." It was a rather comical wording of our long-standing policy, but everyone involved understood perfectly. The two boys who were being bothered stayed on our porch for another 5-10 minutes while the 'tormenters' wandered home.

You may never have thought of your home or yard as holy. But I think it's a great idea to establish the "safe-place policy." Start by talking the idea over with your kids. Sometimes siblings can be terribly abusive to each other. You're going to have to make sure they're supportive of the idea, or the whole system may break down before you ever make the announcement to your neighborhood.

A safe place is where each family member feels free to be open and honest without fear of being judged, criticized, lectured, ridiculed, misunderstood, punished, betrayed, laughed at, or accused.

It takes courage to be vulnerable. A safe environment allows a person to be themselves and voice their thoughts. It's in open dialog that you really get to know yourself and others. Once family trust is shattered by thoughtless words and acts, dishonesty, or disloyalty, it's hard to resurrect. Family members close up to protect themselves. They become secretive and suspicious. This is the worst possible background for successful marriage. Marriage demands complete honesty and self-disclosure in order for true intimacy to be experienced. If marriage partners have been denied this in childhood, the marriage will suffer until the persons get the counseling needed to break through their defenses.

Providing a safe place where no one has to fear the loss of personhood is all a part of keeping the 6th commandment.

Commandment 7: "You shall not commit adultery." That sounds pretty clear, "Don't have sex with anyone but your husband or wife." But that is a far too narrow interpretation of this commandment. According to Jesus, even the first act that breaks down a trust relationship is sinful. "But I say to you that whoever looks at a woman to lust for her has already committed adultery with her in his heart" (Matthew 5:28). Clarke's *Commentary* comments on the seventh commandment, "Not only *adultery* is forbidden here, but also fornication and all kinds of mental and sensual uncleanness. All impure *books, songs, pictures*, etc., which tend to inflame and debauch the mind, are against this law." Can your children trust your home to be a place where evil influences aren't allowed to enter in any way?

Make sure there is no cause for jealousy in your marriage. No marriage is completely affair-proof. It only takes admiring another, noticing qualities that are lacking in your spouse, and realizing that you enjoy spending time together to begin an affair—maybe not a physical one, but a psychological one which can be just as devastating to a marriage. Here's how you can demonstrate your trustworthiness and affair-proof your marriage.

- Never spend time alone with someone of the opposite sex. Even rumors can destroy.
- Don't allow lingering eye contact. It's the beginning of bonding.
- Never touch a person if alone. And avoid a lingering touch in public.
- Don't meet someone outside regular business hours or visit a person alone.
- Never disclose private details about your marriage.
- Don't keep appreciation notes from someone other than your spouse to reread when you're discouraged. Develop

the habit of going to your spouse for support, not to anyone else.

• When someone comes on to you, stop it immediately. Don't flirt with danger just because you enjoy the admiration.

• Talk to your spouse intimately for at least fifteen minutes a day, plan a weekly date together, and an annual "second honeymoon."

Commandment 8: "You shall not steal." Any act of dishonesty breaks down a trust relationship. We must honor property rights and not take something that is not ours. For society to exist at all, this principle must be safeguarded, else there is no security and no protection. All would be anarchy. Any dishonest act that results in us getting something, either directly or indirectly, that belongs to another is wrong. If we misrepresent the quality of a product or conceal defects, this is an act of theft every bit as much as shoplifting or purse snatching. Employers steal when they withhold promised benefits or force employees to work overtime without compensation. Employees steal when they take longer breaks than allowed or waste time talking with friends, or make personal long-distance calls on company phones. It's stealing to conceal something from a customs inspector or to sign over property to a friend when you plan to declare bankruptcy, or to not declare cash income on your tax returns. Are you feeling uncomfortable? Just remember, your children are watching you. You may think you are concealing your dishonesty, but they catch your inconsistencies. Dishonesty undermines trust. If you are dishonest in your dealings with others, what will keep you from treating them in this same way?

Commandment 9: "You shall not bear false witness against your neighbor." In other words, don't lie! Malicious gossip where either the whole truth is not told, or things are misrepresented in such a way as to cast doubt on another's character, is wrong. On the other hand, remaining silent when an innocent person is being maligned is equally sinful. This commandment can be broken by a shrug of the shoulder or by an arching of the eyebrows. Whoever tampers in any way with the exact truth, in order to gain personal advantage or for any other purpose, is guilty of bearing "false witness."

But what about white lies? A reader of my newspaper column, *Dr. Kay's Q&A*, once commented, "My husband is basically an honest person, but I've noticed that he tends to lie when it doesn't hurt anybody, and when it is financially good for him to do so. For example, when we go to some entertainment and the price of the ticket changes when a child is twelve, he'll say our thirteen-year-old is twelve. I'm worried about what his example is saying to our children."

I answered her concern with the following comments:

At one time honesty was an incredibly important value in America. Remember the story about Abe Lincoln walking almost three miles just to return six-and-a-quarter cents (a coin borrowed from Spanish currency and used at that time) that he had overcharged a customer? Most people today wouldn't go as far as the parking lot! In a recent poll, 23% said they would commit a crime for $10 million if they thought they could get away with it! When asked if they would report a $2,000 cash income to the IRS, 45 percent of the respondents earning $50,000 plus said they would cheat—I mean "forget" to report it! And what if they found a wallet with $1000 in it? Respondents aged 18 to 34 were ten times more likely to keep the money than people 65 and older. I personally think the lack of honesty today is deplorable! Who can you trust? For if people are a little dishonest for their own good, what keeps them from further dishonesty—for their own good?

Values, such as honesty, are basically a product of our family of origin. That's why parental example is so important. No two individuals have exactly the same values. The challenge in marriage is to fuse the two value systems in such a way that conflict is minimized, without compromising individual moral standards.

You cannot be responsible for the moral decisions your husband makes, or force him to live by your standards. Each of you must take personal responsibility. Your children are aware of these differences. So, for their benefit openly discuss your value differences with them, pointing out why you make the choices you do and why they should make their own decisions about right or wrong based on principles rather than just blindly following parental example.

Although the highest level of moral decision making is based on unchanging principles, in reality we often make decisions for other reasons. Think about it: Are you honest or dishonest in certain situations because you're scared you'll get caught and be punished? Or do you think the reward for dishonesty is big enough to take a chance? (For example, when you choose to exceed the speed limit, or decide to say nothing when the clerk gives you an extra dollar in change.) Decisions based on punishment or reward are the very lowest level of moral decision making and change with circumstances.

A more mature reason would be to make a moral decision based on whether or not it was the nice thing to do, or the expected thing to do. Conformity to the standards of others or the rules of society is the next level. Although more stable than decisions based on punishment or reward, these decisions will change when society changes. The best and highest standard is to base your decisions on changeless moral principles. These internal standards can't be changed by punishment, reward, or what others think. When people make decisions based on principles, they can be trusted.

Tell your kids as they travel through the jungle of value-laden decisions, the safest way is always the *higher* road!

What would be a principled decision concerning honesty? One might be that trust is essential for meaningful human relationships and dishonesty destroys trust. Or, "Thou shalt not steal—or bear false witness," although given as a moral code thousands of years ago, it did set a standard to ensure that people wouldn't hurt each other.

And don't let anyone kid you, dishonesty always hurts someone! Especially in marriage. A meaningful marriage depends on complete honesty. To have one, you must not hold anything back from the other. You can't keep secrets and be open at the same time. Intimacy requires full disclosure; not necessarily all the details, but no surprises or skeletons in the closet.

Commandment 10: "*You shall not covet your neighbor's house . . . nor anything that is your neighbor's.*" We must be satisfied with what life deals us. Taking a close look at God's Ten Commandments, the last differs from the other nine. The first nine all deal with behavior, the final one digs deeper and looks at motives. Coveting is not an action. It is an inner desire. The lesson is summed up in Proverbs 4:23 "Keep your heart with all diligence, For out of it spring the issues of life." Or as *The Living Bible* puts it, "Above all else, guard your affections. For they influence everything else in your life."

Are you trustworthy?

Do you say what you mean and do what you say? Do you keep the promises you make? Can your children, without a doubt, trust you? I'm excited about the thousands of men who have joined Promise Keepers, an organization of men who are recommitting themselves to God and to keeping the promises they have made to their wives and children. If only everyone was a promise keeper!

Just remember, it's not just the big promises that are important in maintaining a trustworthy relationship. The little ones count more than you might think.

- Do you pick up your child after school when you say you will?
- Do you come home when you're expected?
- Do you take time off to go to special places on the weekends when you say you will?
- When you say, "just a minute" do you mean it?
- Do you stick up for your family in public?

If you break too many promises, your credibility will be questioned and your children won't trust or respect you. Yet parents aren't perfect, and sometimes promises can't be kept. The answer is to make conditional promises, unless you are absolutely sure you can fulfill your word. Conditional promises might be broken if certain conditions exist. "I'll take you swimming if you get your room cleaned and it doesn't rain."

If something happens and it's a hardship to keep a promise, ask permission to break it. "I promised to take you swimming, and I will if you still want to go. But let me explain to you why I think it might be better if we waited until another day." After explaining your reasons for wanting to break your promise, let your child decide what you should do. "You must have your hair cut before we go out for dinner tonight. We could either swim for a short while today, since you need a haircut, or we could wait and go swimming tomorrow for a longer time."

When you feel forced to break a promise to your family, ask yourself if it is really necessary. Chances are you will decide that the good rapport you have with your children by keeping your promises is more important than most reasons you might give for breaking them.

When you say you'll always be there for your family, do you mean it?

In 1989 an 8.2 earthquake devastated Armenia, and in less than four minutes over thirty thousand people died. One of the heart-grabbing stories that came from that disaster is reported by Jack Canfield and Mark Victor Hansen in their book, *Chicken Soup for the Soul*. It's the story of a father searching for his son in the mound of rubble that resulted when the schoolhouse collapsed. The thing that kept him digging was the promise that he had often repeated to his son, "No matter what, I'll always be there for you!"

Other well-meaning parents, mourning for their children buried beneath the rubble, tried to pull him away, saying, "It's too late! They're dead! You can't help! Go home! Come on, face reality, there's nothing you can do!"

But to each parent he responded with one line: "Are you going to help me now?" and then he proceeded to dig for his son, stone by stone.

The fire chief tried to persuade him to go home. Then the police. But he would not listen to their warnings about fires breaking out, the threat of explosions, or their assurance, "We'll handle it!" He asked each to help, but they refused. But because he had made a commitment to his son to always be there, he kept digging. He could not rest until he knew for sure if his son was dead or alive. He dug for eight hours, twelve, twenty-four, thirty-six. Then, in the thirty-eighth hour, he pulled back a stone and heard his son's voice. "Armand!" he screamed.

And in a weak voice his son replied, "Dad? It's me. I told the other kids not to worry. I told 'em that if you were alive, you'd save me, and when you saved me, they'd be saved. There are fourteen of us left out of thirty-three. We're scared, hungry, thirsty, and thankful you're here. When the building collapsed, it made a wedge, like a triangle, and it saved us."

"Come on out, boy!" his father urged.

"No, Dad! Let the other kids out first, 'cause I know you'll get me! No matter what, I know you'll be there for me!"

Do your children, your spouse, or your friends know you'll be there for them? Can your words and actions be trusted? Being trustworthy is the foundation for trust—and trust is a vital part of love.

Chapter Fourteen

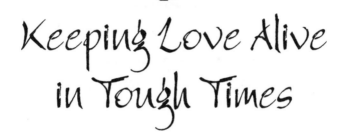

Keeping Love Alive in Tough Times

"Love is never lost,
If not reciprocated, it will flow back
and soften and purify the heart."
—*Washington Irving*

Love is easy to talk about but difficult to practice. In theory, we live so close to the Lord that His love sustains us every hour of the day. In practice, we don't. On many days our ebullient highs are followed by melancholy lows. We soon find ourselves acting out negative feelings. Some fluctuate noticeably between moods. But remember, you can be loving when low by learning how to control your love cup when it's nearly empty.

Being loving is easy when things go well. But what do you do when you've lost your job, your telephone has been disconnected, your dad's dying of cancer, your best friend moved across the country, your sister won't talk to you because of something you said that hurt her feelings, rumors are spreading around the church linking you with something you didn't do, you haven't had any energy for the last four months and a stream of doctors can't find out what's wrong—what do you do when life comes crashing down around you? What do you do when you feel like the older woman in the TV movie, *The Mother*, who cries out in heartbreaking despair, "I'm sixty-six years old, and I don't know what the purpose of it all was. An endless, endless struggle. And for what? For what?" Depression is a heavy emotion that sinks to the bottom of a love cup, and once there, it's tough to dislodge!

Anger is another one of those emotions that can empty your cup. What do you do when your six-year-old uses a marking pen to practice his alphabet on a freshly-painted wall? You spend an hour scrubbing, only to discover that marker pen ink is much more durable than paint. The job is almost done; you check your watch. Oops! Hurry, you'll be late for an appointment. You dash into the bedroom to find the clothes you planned to wear in a rumpled heap on the floor of the closet. Your oldest daughter has been going through your wardrobe again. Your anger is mounting. You yell, "Pick up these clothes immediately!" The response: silence. The culprit has mysteriously disappeared. Then you notice broken china on the floor. The antique vase! You've had it! You confront your toddler. Her response: "Dog did it." No repentance. Is your anger bringing you close to the breaking point? You bet it is!

Back to our metaphorical love cup. In a sense, we are emotional containers. We can hold only so much. When depression, anger, fear, or other negative emotions increase, the more positive ones decrease. Love is usually the emotion to go first. Just when you need it most, you look into your love cup and find it drained.

Perhaps the reason love goes first is because our emotions are tied to our body chemistry. When our love cups are full, when we are experiencing positive relationships with others, endorphins (chemically similar to morphine) flow into our brains, leaving us with a sense of security, peace, and calm. Because we feel no sense of threat, our defenses are lowered, and we can risk loving others.

When we experience a negative emotion, adrenaline floods our system, preparing us to defend ourselves, either by escaping or standing our ground and fighting. Survival becomes the primary motivator. Unfortunately, protecting ourselves has very little to do with having a full love cup. In fact, self-preservation behaviors may cause us to be so defensive and controlling that we alienate ourselves from the very people who could fill us. Behaviors like bossiness, showing off, controlling the conversation, selfishness, and conceit don't win friends and influence people!

You cannot control sudden emotion when it hits. Your body was designed to react emotionally to various circumstances. But if you are perceptive, you can control the negative before it rages out of control.

When you realize your love cup is low, its contents being displaced by other emotions, try these steps:

First, *do a reality check*. Admit you're low. The contents of your love cup will fluctuate, depending upon life circumstances you often can't control. So there is nothing wrong with being low. Staying there is the problem. That's when you slip into a self-preservation mode and withdraw by becoming depressed or begin to deal with others in an unloving way by acting out your negative emotions.

Second, *remember, you have an action choice.* You have the power to refill an empty love cup, including your own. But it won't happen naturally. The natural reaction is to act out your feelings; to treat people as you feel they richly deserve to be treated. The loving reaction is to treat people according to their needs. If they need recognition, give it to them. If they need attention, give it to them. If they need security, give it to them. None of these behaviors comes naturally. That's why love that isn't reciprocated is always a choice. That's why God has commanded us to love one another. He knew it wouldn't come naturally.

Third, *identify the emotion that's threatening your love cup.* What emotion or emotions are trying to force love out of your life? The more specific you can be, the more quickly you can plan your defense strategy. You might want to look back over the list of negative emotions in the "Shrinking the Emotional Giants in Your Life" chapter, to give you insight into what you're feeling at this moment.

Once you have identified the troublesome emotion, admit what you are experiencing. Say, "I am sad," or "I am jealous." Taking ownership of your emotions is the first step in giving yourself permission to do something about them so you can act rationally, independent of your emotions.

Don't fall into the trap of blaming someone or something else for your negative feelings. You own your feelings, and, therefore, you are responsible for them. If your husband walks out the door with a beautiful blonde and leaves you with three kids, you're going to feel rejected. That's understandable. But you don't have to entertain feelings of rage, bitterness, envy, and revenge. That's your choice, and you shouldn't try to escape responsibility for what you're feeling by blaming him! Just because your dad died in the traffic accident when you were driving and you're overcome by guilt, you can't blame the accident for your feelings. If you plateau at the level of blaming situations or others, you will halt the healing process. If you blame others, you will not take the personal responsibility necessary for dealing with troublesome emotions.

Fourth, *not every problem needs to be handled immediately*. Tackle your negative emotions immediately, but not necessarily your problems. In fact, most problems are handled better after you gain control—after your love cup gets refilled. No amount of ranting and raving can put the vase back together again. No amount of pouting or spouting can stop the rumors. If you feel ready to explode with words and actions guaranteed to empty someone else, you need to move immediately to the fifth step.

Fifth, *take positive action to refill your own cup of love*. You cannot fill others from an empty cup. Therefore, it's essential that you learn ways to fill yourself with feelings of contentment and pleasure when there's no one around to give you a quick fix. Take time for a word of prayer, contact the Master Cup Filler. Contact a family member or friend who makes you feel warm inside. Force yourself to reach out and do something loving for someone, anyone, and you'll feel better. Call "time out" and pleasure yourself. Breathe deep and get some exercise. Any of these things will help. When I'm really low, I try them all.

Five successful cup fillers

Cup filler #1: Go to the Master Cup Filler: Read God's Word. God is the Master Cup Filler. So when you're low, why not go to the expert. God's Word has help for every occasion. When I gain insight into the reason for my empty cup, I look for God's promises concerning that problem. For example, if I'm frustrated and need a calm, quiet spirit with a touch of joy, I might turn to Philippians 4:4-8, and I think of the apostle Paul writing these words from that cold, dark Roman dungeon. I'm quickly reminded that things really aren't *that* bad! Here is his counsel and encouragement to me. "Rejoice in the Lord always, Again I will say rejoice! Let your gentleness be known to all men. The Lord is at hand. Be anxious for nothing, but in everything by prayer and supplication, with thanksgiving, let your requests be made known to God; and the peace of God, which surpasses all understanding, will guard your hearts and minds through Christ Jesus." And then as I read, "Finally, brethren, whatever things are *true*, whatever things are *noble*, whatever things are *just*, whatever things are *pure*, whatever things are *lovely*, whatever things are of *good report*, if there is any virtue and if there is anything praiseworthy—meditate on these things," I recall the blessings in my life that fit these positive parameters.

When I can identify the negative emotion that is crowding into my life, I begin searching the Scriptures for specific help, and when I find a verse that speaks to my need, I stop and consider the text and let God's Spirit speak to me. So I won't forget, I write my thoughts down as a letter from God to me. Then I write my response. It's wonderful to go back and read how God's Word has met my specific emotional need so completely. It's a real faith builder. I also mark the text in my Bible with the date, the situation, and the specific emotion that was troubling me—or the cup-filling replacement emotion.

Finding your own scriptural answers brings a special sense of satisfaction. But when your cup is empty and you need help NOW, here is where you can start: If you are . . .

ANGRY and need *control*: Proverbs 19:11; Romans 12:14,

17-21; Ephesians 4:26, 27.

ANXIOUS ABOUT CHILDREN'S SALVATION and need *assurance:* Proverbs 20:7; Isaiah 49:25; Isaiah 54:13.

CONFUSED and need *guidance:* Proverbs 3:6; Isaiah 42:16; Jeremiah 29:11.

DESPERATE and need *help immediately:* Psalm 119:126, 145-149.

DEPRESSED and need *uplifting:* Psalm 38; Psalm 107:6-9; Jeremiah 33:3.

DISCOURAGED and need *hope:* Joshua 1:9; Psalm 1: 1-3; Lamentations 3:21-25.

DOUBTFUL and need *faith:* Psalm 50:14, 15; Jeremiah 32:17; Matthew 17:20, 21.

FEARFUL and need *security:* 2 Kings 6:15-17; Psalm 46:1, 2; Psalm 91).

FINANCIALLY WORRIED and need *reassurance:* Psalm 85:12, 13; Proverbs 22:1; Matthew 6:8, 19-21.

GUILTY and need *forgiveness:* Psalm 25:7-11; Isaiah 1:18; 1 John 1:9.

IMPATIENT or *FRUSTRATED* and need *patience:* Psalm 37:7-9; Psalm 40: 1-3; James 1:1-3.

INSULTED or *HURT* and need *to forgive:* Matthew 5:10-12; Luke 17:3, 4; Ephesians 4:32.

JEALOUS or *ENVIOUS* and need *to accept:* Galatians 6:4, 5; James 3:14-16; 1 John 4:17-19.

LONELY and need *friendship* and *support:* Psalm 139: 7-10; Isaiah 54:10; John 14:15-18.

MOURNFUL and need *comfort:* Psalm 126:5, 6; Isaiah 25:8, 9; 2 Corinthians 1:3, 4.

REJECTED and need *acceptance* and *love:* Zephaniah 3:17; John 3:16; Romans 8:38, 39.

SICK and need *healing:* Psalm 103:2-5; Isaiah 57:18, 19;

2 Corinthians 12:9, 10.

SORROWFUL and need *joy:* Psalm 30:4, 5; Isaiah 55:12; John 16; 20-22.

TEMPTED and need *strength:* Psalm 19:12, 13; 1 Corinthians 10:13; James 1:12.

TIRED and need *rest* and *renewed vitality:* Exodus 20: 8-11; Isaiah 40:31; Matthew 11:28-30.

TROUBLED and need *peace:* Psalm 199:165; Isaiah 26:3; Philippians 4:6-7.

UNDISCIPLINED and need *determination:* Ecclesiastes 9:10; 1 Corinthians 9:24, 26, 27; Colossians 3:23, 24.

WEAK and need *strength:* Nehemiah 8:10b; Isaiah 40:29-31; Philippians 4:13.

WORRIED and need *reassurance:* Psalm 55:22; Isaiah 55:8-11; Philippians 4:19.

WORTHLESS and need *personal value:* Psalm 139:1-6, 13, 14, 17, 18; Jeremiah 1:5; 1 John 3:1a.

To help you in your search for biblical love cup fillers, you'll want to get my book, *Love Cup Fillers from God's Word*, and let this book enrich your devotional life.

Sometimes I can't identify the cause of my emptiness. Then I follow another plan. I know God's love can give me contentment. He knows what I need before I do, so I pick up *The Living Bible*, a modern paraphrase, and turn to Ephesians 3:17-19 and read over and over, "May your roots go down deep into the soil of God's marvelous love; and may you be able to feel and understand, as all God's children should, how long, how wide, how deep, and how high his love really is; and to experience this love for yourselves, though it is so great that you will never see the end of it or fully know or understand it. And so at last you will be filled up with God himself."

I read Paul's prayer as if I were a first-century Ephesian,

as if it were written especially for me. I try to envision how high, wide, and deep God's love really is. I reach the conclusion that I've sealed a tight cover on my cup that's keeping me from receiving His all-encompassing love, and in my imagination I take the cover off my cup and hold it out to the Lord for filling.

Generalized worry sometimes zaps my energy and my ability to go to sleep. Then I rely on my childhood favorite, the twenty-third Psalm, to calm my nerves and put me to sleep. This is an incredible chapter. In just six verses, God reassures me that my every need will be taken care of. It's generic help for worry. I lie in bed and repeat the chapter from memory, then go back to savor every phrase.

"The Lord is my shepherd." Why should I worry if I have the Creator of the universe taking care of me?

"I shall not want." I have lots of wants, but I like the thought in *The Living Bible*. "Because the Lord is my shepherd, I have everything I need." And that's certainly true. I begin to think of my blessings, thanking the Lord for them one by one.

"He makes me to lie down in green pastures;" God will meet my need for a comfortable, safe, and refreshing place to live.

"He leads me beside the still waters." Even though there may be some rough places in my life, God won't allow more troubles to come to me than I can handle. He can find some still water places where I can drink when I'm thirsty and not be afraid.

"He restores my soul." He'll take all my negative emotions—my anxiety, my bitterness, my frustrations—and will give me His peace.

"He leads me in the paths of righteous for His name's sake." He'll even help me make good decisions about what's right and wrong, so I won't have to suffer from the consequences of bad decisions.

"Yea, though I walk through the valley of the shadow of death, I will fear no evil; For You are with me; Your rod and Your staff, they comfort me." I don't even have to be afraid when my life is threatened with harm, pain, sickness, or death. God is my protector.

"You prepare a table before me in the presence of my enemies." I'm not going to have to worry about enough to eat. God has a banquet table prepared for me. God's going to honor me, in front of people who treat me like dirt. He's going to show them I'm really somebody, because I'm His child. That really makes me feel valuable!

"You anoint my head with oil." I'm not even going to have to worry about pain and sickness. He's going to pour His healing oil over me. And since oil is symbolic of the Holy Spirit, I take this as a promise to fill me with His Spirit, His presence, His love, so full that "My cup runs over." By now I'm beginning to relax—and smile in satisfaction and repeat the last verse:

> "Surely goodness and mercy shall follow me
> All the days of my life;
> And I will dwell in the house of the LORD
> Forever."

If all the things mentioned in this psalm are true, I have no business feeling low. I pray, "You've filled my cup in the past, so please, God, fill it now."

Then, as I think of all the good things God has done for me, I begin to feel His love refilling me and in my head (I don't want to wake my husband!) I joyfully shout, "Yes, Yes, Yes!"

When my sense of personal value slips, I turn to Proverbs

31. I skim over the first part of the chapter about the good wife because I don't want to nurture my guilt feelings. Obviously I'm not the perfect woman of the Proverbs! But I do want to identify with the words in Proverbs 31:29. I even read my name into the text. "Many daughters have done virtuously, but you, Kay Kuzma, excel them all."

I don't shout it to the world. I don't even tell my family. It does sound bold and self-righteous. But God said it. And I know that if I could actually hear Him, those words would be His for me. But not only for me, also for you. He made us and loves each of us supremely. I'm sure it is the will of our Creator and Redeemer that we think highly of His creation! In God's sight each of us is to excel in the tasks and responsibilities God has given us to do.

My advice is this: whether you're male or female, whenever you have trouble facing the person in the mirror, strengthen yourself with God's words of Proverbs 31:29, changing the gender if necessary. Read it again and again. God will fill your cup.

I can't emphasize enough the importance of taking time to let God fill your cup when you're low: reading His Word and talking to Him about what you read. The temptation will be to skip this most important step and rush out to do something yourself to fill your cup. But in doing so, you'll miss the greatest source of help in the world!

On an old carbon-copied sheet of paper in my files I came across this letter. Although it was written by an anonymous human hand, let Jesus' words speak to you.

My dear friend,
I just had to send a note to tell you how much I love you and care about you. I saw you yesterday as

you were talking with your friends. I waited all day, hoping you would want to talk with me also. As evening drew near, I gave you a sunset to close your day and a cool breeze to rest you. And I waited. But you never came. It hurt me, but I still love you because I am your friend.

I saw you fall asleep last night and I longed to touch your brow. So, I spilled moonlight on your pillow and your face. Again I waited, wanting to rush down so that we could talk. I have so many gifts for you. But you awakened late the next day and rushed off to work. My tears were in the rain.

Today you looked so sad, so all alone. It makes my heart ache because I understand. My friends let me down and hurt me so many times too. But I love you. Oh, if you would only listen to me. I really love you, I try to tell you in the blue sky and in the quiet green grass. I whisper it in the leaves on the trees and breathe it in the colors of the flowers. I shout it to you in the mountain streams and give the birds love songs to sing. I clothe you with warm sunshine and perfume the air with nature's scents. My love for you is deeper than the oceans and bigger than the biggest want or need in your heart.

If you only knew how much I want to help you. I want you to meet my Father. He wants to help you, too. My Father is that way, you know. Just call me, ask me, talk with me. I have so much to share with you. But, I won't hassle you. I'll wait, because I love you.

Your Friend,
Jesus

Cup filler #2: Reach out to your family and friends. God has helpers who are pleased to do some filling. But often they don't know whose cup needs love. If I have a need, it's my responsibility to let them know: "I'm empty." No one has ever turned me down when I've asked. There's been some mumbling and fumbling and, "Tell me what to do," but the spirit was always one of wanting to help. So, when I'm low, I contact someone who can encourage me.

I'm especially blessed because God provided me with a husband who's a born cup filler. Most mornings his greeting is, "It's a beautiful day; wonderful things are about to happen!" You can't stay downhearted for long when you live with a bundle of optimism. Jan also has a special concern for me that he carries daily to the Lord. It feels good when you know you are on someone's daily prayer list. Recently he read that for optimum health each person needs eighteen hugs a day. I don't know how scientific that is, but it sure feels good when you're down. All I have to do is look a little discouraged and he gives me another snuggle!

I'm also willing to reach out to others for encouragement. That's why I'm so glad God has provided Christian coworkers and a church family to nurture and sustain me. Sometimes when there's an important meeting in the offing, or a key decision coming up, I'll ask a colleague to pray for me.

My friends are especially important. I need energy to get through my long list of daily tasks. The counterforces of unhappiness, discouragement, and negativism deplete my energy and make me tired. So I choose my closest friends with care: optimistic people. I need every one of them; when I'm experiencing a low I'll give a call to Jill, Dick, Dianne, Katie, or Elden. We may not discuss my problem; just their cheerfulness and enthusiasm gives me the boost I need.

Creating Love

In return, I encourage them to call me. Each day I ask the Lord to let me know who needs their cup filled, and when I have an impression to call someone or write, I've learned to act on it!

Here's a little poem that was sent to me by one of my cup-filling friends. I have no idea who wrote it, but it filled me and I hope you'll pass it along to fill others.

> I said a prayer for you today
>> And know God must have heard.
> I felt the answer in my heart
>> Although He spoke no word!
> I didn't ask for wealth or fame.
>> (I knew you wouldn't mind.)
> I asked Him to send treasures
>> Of a far more lasting kind!
> I asked that He'd be near you
>> At the start of each new day,
> To grant you health and blessings,
>> And friends to share your way!
> I asked for happiness for you,
>> In all things great and small,
> But it was for His loving care
>> I prayed for most of all!

Cup filler #3: Do something loving for someone else. Servant love is another way to help God fill your cup. You see, love has a mysterious property. You can't give it away without getting it back. In fact, I once read that one of the most difficult things to give away is kindness, for it is usually returned!

So think about those who need love and attention more than you. Whose life could you touch with a little sunshine and happiness? Perhaps you could pick a bouquet of flowers, bake cookies or bread for a neighbor, or send a note.

This way of filling your own cup works especially well when you are feeling unloving toward someone. Instead of following your first impulse, turn the page and do something nice like the old Quaker in this nineteenth-century parable called *The Quaker's Corncrib*.

A certain man had been in the habit of stealing corn from his Quaker neighbor. Every night he would tiptoe to the corncrib and fill his bag with the ears that the good old Quaker's toil had placed there. Every morning the old gentleman observed the shrinking of his corn pile. This was annoying and must be stopped, he thought. But how? Many a person would have suggested, "Take a gun, conceal yourself, wait till he comes, and fire." Others would have said, "Catch the villain and have him sent to jail."

But the Quaker was not prepared to resort to such severe measures. He wanted to punish the offender, but to do it gently enough to bring about reformation if possible. So the Quaker rigged a sort of trap inside the hole through which the man would thrust his arm in getting the corn.

At the hour of midnight the wicked neighbor made his unholy rounds, thrusting his hand into the crib to seize an ear. Suddenly he found himself unable to withdraw it. In vain he tugged, pulled, and alternately cried and cursed. Every effort to release himself only made his hand more secure in the trap.

After a time he gave up his useless struggle and began to look around. All was silent. The rest of the world slept quietly while he was compelled to keep a dreary, humiliating watch through the remainder of the long night, his hand in constant pain from the pressure of the clamp that held it. He stood and watched the progress of the night and simultaneously desired and dreaded the arrival of morning.

It came at last. The Quaker looked out his window and found that he had caught his man. What was to be done? Some would have said, "Go out and give a good whipping just as he stands, and then release him. That'll cure him." But that was not the Quaker's plan. Such a course would have sent the man away embittered and muttering curses of revenge. That kindly old Quaker hurriedly dressed, then went to relieve and to punish his prisoner.

"Good morning, friend," said he as he came within speaking distance. "How does thee do?"

The poor culprit made no answer but burst into tears.

"I'm sorry that thee has gotten thy hand caught," said the Quaker as he proceeded to release the man. "Thee put it in the wrong place, or it would not have been so."

The culprit looked crestfallen and, begging forgiveness, hastily turned to make his retreat. "Stay," said his persecutor—for he was now becoming such to the thief, who could have received a blow easier than the gracious words that were falling from the Quaker's lips. "Stay, friend; thy bag is not filled. Thee needs corn, or thee would not have taken so much pains to get it. Come, let us fill the bag." The poor fellow was obliged to stand and hold the bag while the old man filled it, interspersing the exercise with the pleasantest conversation imaginable. When the bag was full, the embarrassed thief once more muttered his apologies and thanks and tried to leave, but once more the Quaker stopped him.

"Stay, friend," said the Christian again. "Ruth has breakfast ready. Thee must not think of going without breakfast. Come, Ruth is calling!"

The Quaker was "heaping coals" with a vengeance (see Romans 12:20, 21). Without success, the mortified neighbor begged to be excused from what to him would be a punishment ten times worse than a beating and imprisonment. But the Quaker insisted.

After breakfast was over, the old farmer said to his dishonest neighbor, "Now if thee need any more corn, come in the daytime, and thee shall have it." With what shame and remorse did that guilty man turn from the dwelling of the forgiving Quaker!

Everybody is ready to say that the thief never again troubled the Quaker's corncrib. But I have something still better to tell you. The thief experienced conversion that day and, according to one who heard him relate the substance of the preceding story in a church meeting, attributed his change of living to the actions of his Christian neighbor, to arrest him on his downward course. —*Author Unknown*

What would you have done if your neighbor was stealing your corn? And going back to the beginning of the chapter and putting yourself in the shoes of the distraught parent, what could you do for the children who wrote on the wall, messed up your closet, and broke your vase? Of course they need certain consequences so they can learn more appropriate behavior, but they might also benefit from a love note, an offer to help clean their rooms, or a piece of their favorite pie for dessert. Better yet, give them some of your precious time.

A father once related a story about his teenage son who had hardly spoken to him in months. They lived in the same house, but communication was almost nonexistent. The son was punishing his father with silence. Whenever the father tried to get him to speak, matters became worse.

The father found an expensive ten-speed racing bike on sale. His son had always wanted one, but it was something that he had never felt necessary. Suddenly, an impulse! Why not buy it? He did.

When the son saw the bike, he asked coldly, "Whose bike?"

"Yours," the father replied.

His son was dumbfounded. "For me? Why? I don't deserve a bike!"

The boy was overwhelmed with his father's kindness. His resistance collapsed. He couldn't contain his feelings. He ran to his father and hugged him. The strike was over.

As the father told the story, he admitted it might have been an illogical thing to do. But it was an effective means to fill his son's love cup. By showing love he reaped a bountiful harvest.

You can be effective in filling your own love cup if you reach out to God and to others and accept the love they are so willing to give. "Ask and you shall receive" is good advice. Another way of putting it might be, "Fill another's love cup and you shall be filled."

Cup filler # 4: Take care of your health and physical needs. Have you been taking good care of yourself? Do you daily eat a good breakfast and get some exercise—the kind that makes your heart work and releases those little endorphins that give you a natural high? A gynecologist once commented to me that most women's depressions could be overcome with a daily thirty-minute brisk walk in the fresh air!

Have you had a good physical exam recently to make sure there isn't a medical problem causing your feelings of apathy and depression? Our bodies are such intricate mechanisms that even a slight chemical or hormonal imbalance can throw us all out of kilter. Sometimes hidden allergies can zap our physical and emotional energy. If negative feelings persist, don't hesitate to ask for a psychiatric referral, because psychiatrists are the arm of the medical team who not only have an intimate knowledge of mental disorders but can also prescribe various drugs to help bring your body chemistry back into balance, if that's the problem.

Maybe your love cup empties, and you end up emptying others, on a monthly cycle. Does your husband lament, "PMS makes my wife impossible to live with. Nothing pleases her. Everything I say is wrong. I just try to stay out of her way until it's over." Premenstrual Syndrome can have a devastating effect on a woman's life and her marriage.

But the good news is that PMS can be helped or hindered by your lifestyle, particularly by diet, says Dr. Susan Lark, who wrote *The Premenstrual Syndrome Self-Help Book*. Here are the foods to avoid: alcohol and caffeinated beverages; dairy products, chocolate, and sugar. Stay away from beef, pork, and lamb. And avoid salt and high sodium foods such as bouillon, commercial salad dressings, catsup and hot dogs, chips, and tropical fruits like oranges, papaya, and pineapple.

Instead, you'll want to eat the foods that help neutralize PMS: whole grains, legumes, seeds and nuts, vegetables, and fruits from temperate climate regions, such as apples, plums, pears, and cherries.

But regardless if PMS is a problem in your life or not, I'll guarantee you'll feel better if you avoid alcohol, caffeinated beverages, animal and dairy products, chocolate, sugar, salt, fried and processed foods. And you can't go wrong with whole grains, legumes, seeds and nuts, vegetables and fruits, and plenty of good drinking water! Purchase a book of healthful recipes, and you'll be delighted with how tasty foods can be when prepared without fat, sugar, and animal products.

One of the best things you can do for your love cup, and those of your family members, is to improve your lifestyle. When you feel better, you treat others better and, in turn, they'll treat you better.

Cup filler #5: Do something to pleasure yourself. There is nothing wrong with taking some time to pleasure yourself. You can't fill others if your own cup is empty. Have you been so busy helping others that you've neglected yourself? You can't run on empty for long without breaking down.

Most mothers I talk to say that, "Not enough time," is the biggest problem in their lives. There's not enough time for the family, and certainly no time for personal pleasures.

But that's not true. You can find time for yourself if you choose. Even Jesus, in His hectic schedule where He and His disciples didn't even have time to eat because of the hundreds who so desperately needed them, said, "Come aside by yourselves to a deserted place and rest a while." If you're overworked, Jesus is talking to you.

Where would that deserted place be in your life? And what would you want to do with that gift of time that would bring you renewed energy and contentment?

I like to grab a good book and read. I also enjoy making silk flower arrangements—but our home can only display so many! So I've already made Christmas wreaths for my family and friends for next year! I also enjoy the release I feel when I finally finish a long overdue project. And I love a l-o-n-g shower or bubbly bath. That's contentment!

But my biggest pleasure is the freedom of a weekly Sabbath. I've been given Divine permission every seven days to not think about anything work-related (either at the office or at home) for a whole twenty-four hours. Can you imagine? An entire twenty-four-hour period with my Creator, where I can rest and not have any guilt feelings about what I'm not accomplishing! It's kind of like walking into heaven! And by the way, you've been given the same gift, tucked neatly in the middle of God's Ten Commandments (see Exodus 20:8-11). Don't leave it wrapped on the shelf. Enjoy it—you need it for maximum productivity and a full cup. Don't cheat yourself.

In addition to a weekly time-out period, we all need a piece of time each day for ourselves. We all need private places where we can put ourselves back together without phone calls, door bells, and TV disturbing us. And we all need projects, interests, and hobbies that bring us a sense of satisfaction and a reminder of our competence.

What fills your cup? If you had a twenty-four-hour piece of time with no obligations and responsibilities, what would you do? Now take that dream and break it into little pieces and scatter some minivacations throughout your week, and the contentment level of your love cup will be more easily maintained.

You are a son or daughter of a King. Treat yourself like royalty, even if others forget. "Behold what manner of love the Father (the King of the Universe) has bestowed on us, that we should be called children of God!" (1 John 3:1a).

Chapter Fifteen

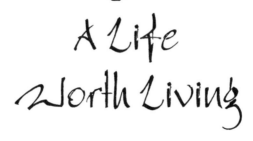

A Life Worth Living

"Take away love and our earth is a tomb."
—Robert Browning

Cliff started life with the same chance as most other children. A mother, a father, a healthy body, fine potential, and a love cup ready to be filled. His problem: finding someone to fill it.

Cliff was a shy, sensitive, fair-haired boy whose life began to crumble when he was in second grade. His parents, whom he loved, got a divorce. He was sad and hurt. He became so depressed that he couldn't keep his mind on his teacher's words. The print in his book seemed blurred, and the numbers on the page didn't add up. His teacher was concerned. She saw that Cliff was falling behind his classmates. She approached him gently. "Cliff, how can I help you?" Without thinking, she added, "You know, you're the slowest child in the class." She meant only to be helpful, but her careless words staggered Cliff. Now he had to deal both with conflict at home and failure at school.

His classmates all seemed happy and bright. At least they appeared so to Cliff. They quickly picked up ideas that his troubled mind was slow to absorb. He felt left out and alone. He withdrew.

Cliff was afraid to make friends, afraid of rejection. To him it seemed safer just to wait for someone else. He waited. But no one said, "Hi, Cliff. Come play with me."

Cliff never invited anyone to his house. He knew what might happen. His mother had remarried; his stepfather drank heavily, and Cliff never knew what to expect. He certainly couldn't explain this to a playmate. Instead, Cliff silently complied with his stepfather's orders. Cliff resented the man. He would have liked to spend more time with his mother, but she, too, was usually hustling to meet the stepfather's demands.

Years passed. Cliff lived in a home devoid of parental affection. His teachers lost interest. He was merely a warm body in the classroom. No one seemed to care.

He was twelve years old when life turned unbearable. One winter's day he was watching some boys building a snowman. In a feeble voice he asked, "May I help?"

They turned on Cliff like a pack of wolves. They taunted, "Well, if it isn't Cliff Evans! We don't need your help!" One boy grabbed Cliff's hat and threw it to his buddy. They played "keep away." Back and forth they tossed the hat as Cliff tried to recover it. Finally, the biggest boy pushed Cliff into a snow bank, ceremoniously put the hat on the snowman's head, and named the snowman, "Dumb Cliff."

The same day, Cliff took the long way home, found some budding pussy willow branches, and arrived late. He thought the pussy willows might please his mother and even his stepfather. Instead, the stepfather was irate. "Where have you been?" he yelled, "I told you to shovel the walk!" He slapped Cliff, knocking the pussy willows from his hand.

The next morning Cliff felt ill. He didn't want to go to school and be teased. Yet he didn't want to stay home and be slugged. Miserable, he boarded the school bus. The kids were happily talking. Everyone else had a friend. He was ignored. They acted as if he didn't exist. Moments later, overcome with pain, he made his way up the aisle of the bus and said, "I got to get off!"

The driver yelled at him, "You just got on—I can't let you off!" But at the next stop, he opened the door, Cliff stumbled down the steps and fell down in the snow. Cold. Alone. He died of an empty cup. Life just wasn't worth living.

It's a tragic story—documented in Brigham Young University's film, *Cipher in the Snow*. I showed the film to a children's church group. In the discussion that followed, I asked the children, "Do any of you know a Cliff Evans in your school?"

No one answered. Everyone looked at their shoes. Was the silence an expression of guilt? I knew how thoughtless children could be to one another. No doubt most of these had at some time hurt, teased, or ignored another youngster.

I asked again: "Is there a Cliff Evans in your school?"

More silence. At last, nine-year-old Cindy raised her hand. "Yes, it's me," she said in a small voice. "I feel like Cliff every day I go to school."

I couldn't believe it. I had known Cindy for two years. She had been in my special discussion group at children's church each week, and I had no inkling of her bruised feelings and empty cup.

I determined that I would help Cindy. I would fill her love cup and give her hope. A few weeks later, Cindy's chair was empty. Her family had suddenly moved. No one knew where; there was no forwarding address.

Cindy is out there. There are millions of Cindys and Cliffs stumbling through an indifferent world, waiting for someone to notice them, someone to care, someone to give them hope and a reason for living.

Teaching Children to be Cup Fillers to Peers

Kari was in fifth grade when she came home from school with disturbing news. Luke, who liked to act tough, had kicked in the spokes on Shirush's bike, and he had had to walk the ruined bike three miles to his sister's home. What caused the trouble? A fit of temper? No, merely the final cup-emptying gesture of a bully who had singled Shirush out as his victim. It was at the time of the Iran hostage affair and Shirush had the misfortune of being from Tehran. He had come over to visit his sister before the hostages were taken, and now it wasn't safe to return, nor could his folks join him in this country. In addition, his name was strange, his language peculiar, and he was short and gentle. A perfect target for abuse.

I talked to the teacher. She confirmed she was having a hard time controlling the words and actions of a few kids in the class. I suggested showing the film, *Cipher in the Snow.* The day it was shown, Shirush's sister kept him home, which gave his classmates an opportunity to discuss what they were doing to Shirush. The film was shocking to the kids. They had no idea how their words and actions were slowly killing this gentle lad who was innocently caught in this unfortunate situation.

The next day Kari reported, "Mom, you'll never believe

what Luke (the bully) did today during recess!"

I feared to hear more.

"Luke loves to play soccer. But in the middle of the game, he noticed Shirush all by himself playing marbles on the sidelines. So he left the game and went over to him and asked if he could play marbles with him."

I breathed a sigh of relief. I wondered if this drama would have been played out in an adult world, would we have been so generous? Would we have made such an about face when confronted with our cup-emptying behavior? Or would we have stubbornly defended ourselves? Another reminder of the truism that we should become as little children. "Therefore whoever humbles himself as this little child is the greatest in the kingdom of heaven" (Matthew 18:4).

We have a responsibility to model cup-filling behavior to our children. What a lesson for a nation when news commentator Connie Chung tricked Newt Gingrich's mother into whispering what Newt, the newly elected Republican Speaker of the House, thought about Hillary Rodham Clinton, wife of the Democratic President. "She's a bitch" was broadcast loudly for the whole world to hear. How did Hillary respond to these cup-emptying words? She invited Newt's mom and dad to the White House, saying she knew how it felt when the news media made public a mistake that was highly embarrassing.

Would we have been so gracious? The sobering fact is, our children will grow up treating others pretty much the way we have treated others. If we want to change the world, we've got to first start with ourselves. Then we must teach the younger generation about how love creates love. Tell them about the love cup and how to fill their peers' cups. Let your parting words to your children each morning be, "Find someone who needs a friend, and be one." When your children return home, ask them, "Whose love cup did you fill today?"

You must also teach them how easy it is to empty someone's cup. When a child is different, or appears defenseless, it makes others feel insecure. If someone takes advantage of this person and teases or threatens, it frightens others. At that moment, the safe side to be on is the bully's. To stick up for the teased would only be an invitation to be persecuted. Explain that bit of psychological theory to your children, so they can understand why it is so hard for them to fill someone when others are emptying. Talk about what they should do if they see someone being hurt, teased, or ignored. Role play solutions. Cup-filling children grow up to be cup-filling adults who can make a difference in the lives of their friends and family and make this world a better place to live.

Love: A reason to live

What is it that makes life worth living? A new car? A stylish wardrobe? A video recorder? New wallpaper? Wealth?

You can be short on material possessions, you can lose your wealth, but somehow you'd manage. You can sustain yourself through a famine. You can survive privation in the wilderness. You can overcome persecution, wars, and riots. You can recover from debilitating disease. You can live a subsistence life with few material benefits. But you can't live a worthwhile life without meaningful human relationships.

A loving relationship is basic; more so than wealth, more so than material comforts. Love sustains your hope for something better. With love you can feel good about yourself. Without love there is no hope. Without love you feel worthless.

Regrettably, too many people suffer from a serious condition: chronically empty love cups. Daily life to them is meaningless. They feel worthless and devoid of hope. This fact is starkly documented by our shocking suicide statistics.

More and more empty people are choosing death as a way out. Suicide is the second leading killer among young people fifteen to twenty-four years of age. And if the underlying cause of many accidental deaths were known, it might possibly emerge as the top culprit. Even young children are not immune. It's eighth on the list of killers of school-age youngsters. Fifty years ago it was almost unknown in this age group.

You might expect the poverty-stricken, those in financial straits, to be the ones who would choose suicide as a way of escaping an unbearable life. The surprising fact is that the affluent, especially affluent teenagers, are significantly at risk.

A number of years ago *The Wall Street Journal* sought an answer for this problem from a number of professionals. Dr. Mary Giffin, a child psychiatrist who at the time practiced in the prosperous north Chicago suburbs where teenage suicide was epidemic, said, "Many of the children (taking their lives) were high achievers and socially adept, not the sort you usually associate with the act. We can only conclude that we are raising children who have very fragile personalities, kids who can be devastated by the slightest setback."

Dr. Lee Salk, a New York clinical psychologist, said, "The material success of parents can be a detriment to child-raising if it comes at the expense of time that should be spent with their children. Children can tell fairly young what their parents consider important. If they see that everything comes ahead of them, there's likely to be trouble ahead."

Dr. Bennett L. Leventhal, director of the Child Psychiatric Clinic at the University of Chicago Medical School, felt that some parents, being unsure of their own values, were unable to offer their children any goals beyond material success. "The kids perceive their parents' expectations that they'll succeed, but not much else. Too often, they grow up lacking the internal controls they need to keep on course."

What are the factors that cause children to take their own lives? According to these experts, the contributing factors include: a fragile personality devastated by problems; lack of parental time and attention, which engenders a feeling that everything else is more important to parents; and lack of parental guidance to instill worthwhile values and goals.

In a way, these factors can be summarized into one relational need—the need to feel loved. Hand in hand with love is hope—the hope that is with you when your life is filled with love.

When you give your love, you give time and attention. And love creates love; it instills within the beloved the desire to share love with others. Filling another's love cup is a goal worth striving for! When your love cup is filled, you don't easily succumb to minor setbacks. Love provides a cushion for the rough spots in life. Love permits you to bounce back.

Why not determine that you'll be a love cup filler to your family and friends? As you do, you'll radiate happiness, and in return, your own love cup will be filled to overflowing, for love defies natural law. The more you give away; the more you will have. And when you're low and you have no one who seems to care, there is an endless supply from which you can freely draw. All you have to do is say, "Fill my love cup, Lord."

> "And now abideth, faith, hope, love,
> these three; but the greatest of these is love."
> —1 Corinthians 13:13

You can contact Kay Kuzma
about speaking engagements or seminars at:

Family Matters
PO Box 7000
Cleveland, TN 37320
1-800-309-LOVE (5683)

Love-Cup Fillers From God's Word

Compiled by Kay Kuzma

Bible texts are from the New King James Version, unless specified.

Creating Love

INTRODUCTION

I'm usually an upbeat person, but it doesn't happen naturally. The example of my folks helped. Dad, especially, always saw the best in everyone, and even in hard times, he never lost hope.

But that's not enough to keep me up!

My husband helps. Jan has an incredible foundation of faith that he established from his childhood days living in Poland when the Nazi's were determined to wipe Poland and its people from the maps of Europe. His faith was further grounded in experiences that his family encountered whle escaping from the clutches of communism.

But that's not enough for me either!

If I am to remain up, I have to have my own experience. I'm sensitive. Things don't automatically roll off me like water off a duck's back. I thrive on accolades and hit bottom when criticized. I can get 1,000 wonderful letters saying how helpful the advice was I gave in my newspaper columns or on my Got a Minute for your Family? radio programs, and then I get one critical letter or phone call, and I fall apart.

Since I never know when I'm going to get slammed in the face with a "cold prickly," I try to keep my psychological immune system healthy, so I don't succumb to anger, depression, or fear when bad things happen. Like taking a daily vitamin, I've made it a practice to search God's Word for the promises that can fill my life with love-cup fillers.

My preventive method is to start reading in the Scriptures, anywhere, and read until I find something that speaks to me for the needs of the day. Then I mark that passage and write it in a journal, along with the special Holy Spirit message I got from that verse.

But when something negative hits, I need specific medication for my specific problem. That's when I go to my concordance and look up help for the emotions that are trying to crowd out that feeling of contentment that I have when my love cup is full. Then I mark those texts and journal.

Now I bring to you the results of my Scriptural search for love-cup fillers. Keep this book with you. You never know when you'll get a speeding ticket and feel worthless, receive notification of an IRS audit and feel discouraged, lose a friend and feel mournful, or be in a threatening storm and feel fearful. But wherever you are, immediate help is available. God has not left us defenseless in this world of hostile emotions. But you'll never believe it until you experience God's filling power yourself.

My prayer for you is one of my favorite cup fillers. "May your roots go down deep into the soil of God's marvelous love; and may you be able to feel and understand . . . how long, how wide, how deep, and how high his love really is. . . . And so at last you will be filled up with God himself" (Ephesians 3:17-19, TLB).

With God's abundant love,
Kay Kuzma

P.S. I use two Bibles to help me keep full. My basic guide is the New King James Version. Because it's so close to the King James Version, it's easy for me to recognize passages I memorized as a child. Plus, I like the poetic sound and the style of the Psalms and Proverbs in this version. For inspirational reading, I enjoy The Living Bible. The modern language grabs me and allows me to see things more clearly. Occasionally, I'll check other versions, and I invite you to do the same.

LOVE-CUP FILLERS FROM GOD'S WORD

Your love cup

You have a love cup: not one of china, silver, or gold, but one deep inside that measures your level of contentment. When life is rich and full, your love cup bubbles over and you are eager to share with others from the abundance of your life. It's easy to give love when you're full to overflowing. But when troubles hit and heavy negative feelings push out those more positive ones from your cup, emptiness invades you and colors your thoughts and actions. Your whole being switches from an offensive game plan where you are reaching out in a loving way to others to a defensive one where you play for survival, trying in every way possible to fill your own cup at the expense of others. Your thoughts center on self; you talk about yourself; you become bossy, demanding, obnoxious. You act selfishly and appear to others to be conceited. You put others down to make yourself look better. You use others for your own gain. And in the process you empty others. It's a lose, lose situation. You end up with even less love, and so do those around you.

But there is another way. To reach out to the Master Cup Filler and say, "Lord, fill my cup. . . ." Fill it up with love.

Why you need spiritual cup fillers

Satan is the thief that is trying to steal space in your love cup, kill your hope, and destroy positive relationships that are natural cup fillers. But Jesus says, " 'I have come that they may have life, and that they may have it more abundantly' " (John 10:10). And to experience an overflowing love cup is to experience life at its best.

Creating Love

You want to live the abundant life, but it's difficult in a world where the devil is going around like a roaring lion seeking to devour the contents of your love cup and leave you emotionally bruised and bleeding.

God, however, has not left you defenseless in this world that threatens to drain your love cup and keep you limping along—or dying—on empty. He has given you wisdom and power through His Holy Spirit to say to the enemy, "Get thou behind me, Satan" when you feel overcome with negative emotions, which are taking up precious space in your love cup. Here's how you can get rid of the negative and fill your cup with God's positive gifts of love, joy, peace, longsuffering, kindness, goodness, faithfulness, gentleness, and self-control.

Instructions:

Step 1: Identify the negative emotion and admit its presence. Say: "I am _____" (negative emotion).

When you feel overcome by a persistent negative emotion, don't try to outrun it. Negative emotions always win. Instead, stop immediately and identify the specific negative emotion that is harassing you and call it by name. Say, "I am angry." Or "I am jealous." Or whatever the negative feeling might be.

Remember, negative emotions don't always present themselves clearly. The devil is smart. If he can disguise the emotion so it can't be easily recognized, it will have a better chance of getting a good hold on the victim, before the victim is even aware of its presence. To deny that you are experiencing an emotion allows it to grow from something small and easily managed to something that ends up controlling you and has such a stranglehold that it appears almost impossible to shake off.

Step 2: Tell the Lord all about it. In other words, be honest and spill your guts out to the Lord. It's best to do this in writing. It's a symbolic act to transfer the negative feeling from your internal love cup to an external piece of paper. For example:

Dear Lord, I am so discouraged! I've disappointed myself and my folks. I feel like a failure because I flunked an exam. I made some stupid errors because I didn't read the questions carefully, and now I'm in this pit of discouragement and can't seem to get out. I can't seem to make myself study for the next exam; I just feel like giving up. I try to think about other things, but this awful empty feeling gnaws at the pit of my stomach, and I keep saying to myself, "I'm so stupid. Why? Why? Why?" I need help. I need hope that this feeling will go away and that I won't freak out the next time I take an exam and flunk again. Your discouraged child . . .

Step 3: Ask God to give you a message that will quickly replace the void in your cup so other negative emotions don't come rushing in to take its place.

Step 4: Read through the texts given under the category that pertains to your need, praying that God will speak to you. Note: the texts given in this book are only an example of the hundreds of texts that are hidden in God's Word. If you find a helpful text among those chosen to be listed here, praise the Lord that your search was easy. But remember, you will tend to appreciate a Bible text more if you have to dig for it. So you might want to move on to Step 5 now.

Step 5: Open your Bible and begin reading until you find a text that speaks to you. To keep a list of helpful texts for future reference, write the complete text under the category it pertains to.

Step 6: Once you have found a text with a message for you, it is important to let God speak to you through the text. In other words, meditate on the text. Open your mind to God's Holy Spirit. Ask Him to bring thoughts to you that are Holy Spirit thoughts straight from the throne of God.

Step 7: Write the thoughts down as they come to you. If you don't, you'll forget. And as you write, you'll find other related thoughts coming to mind. Keep writing. Record these Holy Spirit thoughts as a direct message to you from God. Preface them with "My dear child" and write as if this were God's letter to you. For example, let's say you're discouraged because you've flunked an exam and need some encouragement or hope. The text you discover is Mark 10:27: " 'With men it is impossible, but not with God; for with God all things are possible.' " This might be God's letter to you.

My dear child, I know you are discouraged. I know all about the failed exam. But listen to My words, "With Me all things are possible." We are a team, you and Me. And we are going to do great things together in the future. But you can't go about living your life by yourself and then expect Me to rescue you at the last minute. All things are possible with Me, but for your own good I won't work miracles that will usurp all the responsibility from your shoulders that will help you understand how competent and valuable you are. If I know your life will be happier in the future if you learn some lessons about how to live in the present, then I want you to learn those lessons. Your job is to trust Me that I know what I'm doing in your life. All things are possible if we work as a team. All things are possible if you will do these things to glorify Me instead of glorifying yourself. All things are possible if it is for your good. All things are possible—but you persist in asking Me and being open to My guidance, so I can persist in directing you in the way I want you to go. With all My love, Your Lord and Savior.

Step 8: Write your response to God in a letter to Him. For example:

Dear Lord, I want so badly to believe You when You say that "With You all things are possible," but I've made such a mess of my life. This was such an important exam, and I thought I gave it my best shot. But now I realize that I was trying to do it by myself. I was so busy studying for the last two days I didn't even take time to consult You. I can see now that if I would have passed, I wouldn't have given You any credit. Help me to be a quick learner. I don't like the feeling of discouragement that comes when I feel like a failure. Teach me what I need to do to prepare for future exams so I can experience Your promise "With You all things are possible." Help me to hold on to this promise when I feel like giving up. Here's what I've learned from this experience: All things are possible if I am willing to work with You as a team. All things are possible if I am willing to give You the glory. All things are possible if it's for my own good. (I'm glad You won't work miracles for me that in the end would be a bad thing.) All things are possible if I ask and am open to Your guidance as to what I should do. I feel stronger now. I have hope that with You all things are possible in the future.

Love, Your special friend . . .

Step 9: Mark the text in your Bible. When you find a particularly helpful verse, mark it with the date, situation, and emotion that you were trying to overcome—or gain. For example, you might feel really discouraged and in your search come across Mark 10:27. Beside this text mark the date 10/5/95. Write "failed exam" for the situation. Then write either "Discouraged" for the emotion you want to get rid of or "Hope" for the emotion with which you want to fill your love cup. In this way, when discouragement hits you again, you can easily find the text where God spoke to you and find encouragement once again.

Step 10: If you are dealing with a persistent negative emotion, write on cards the helpful text you found and put them in places where you will be continually reminded of the message. For example, place it on the dash of your car, on the mirror in the bathroom, on the refrigerator door, or on your computer screen.

BIBLE HELP FOR TROUBLESOME EMOTIONS

ANGRY and need control

Be angry, and do not sin. Meditate within your heart on your bed, and be still (Psalm 4:4).

Cease from anger, and forsake wrath; do not fret—it only causes harm (Psalm 37:8; read surrounding verses).

He who is slow to wrath has great understanding, but he who is impulsive exalts folly (Proverbs 14:29).

A soft answer turns away wrath, but a harsh word stirs up anger (Proverbs 15:1).

The discretion of a man makes him slow to anger, and it is to his glory to overlook a transgression (Proverbs 19:11).

"Therefore if you bring your gift to the altar, and there remember that your brother has something against you, leave your gift there before the altar, and go your way. First be reconciled to your brother, and then come and offer your gift" (Matthew 5:23, 24).

Bless those who persecute you; bless and do not curse. . . . Repay no one evil for evil. Have regard for good things in the sight of all men. If it is possible, as much as depends on you, live peaceably with all men. Beloved, do not avenge yourselves, but rather give place to wrath; for it is written, "Vengeance is Mine, I will repay," says the Lord. "Therefore if your enemy hungers, feed him; if he thirsts, give him a drink; for in so doing you will heap coals of fire on his head." Do not be overcome by evil, but overcome evil with good (Romans 12:14;17-21). If someone mistreats you because you are a Christian, don't curse him; pray that God will bless him. . . . Never pay back evil for evil. Do things in such a way that everyone can see you are honest clear through. Don't quarrel with anyone. Be at peace with everyone, just as much as possible.Dear friends, never avenge yourselves. Leave that to God, for he has said that he will repay those who deserve it. [Don't take the law into your own hands.] Instead, feed your enemy if he is hungry. If he is thirsty give him something to drink and you will be "heaping coals of fire on his head." In other words, he will feel ashamed of himself for what he has done to you. Don't let evil get the upper hand but conquer evil by doing good (Romans 12:14; 17-21 TLB).

"Be angry, and do not sin"; do not let the sun go down on your wrath, nor give place to the devil (Ephesians 4:26, 27),

Stop being mean, bad-tempered and angry. Quarreling, harsh words, and dislike of others should have no place in your lives (Ephesians 4:31, TLB).

And now a word to you parents. Don't keep on scolding and nagging your children, making them angry and resentful. Rather, bring them up with the loving discipline the Lord himself approves, with suggestions and godly advice (Ephesians 6:4, TLB).

Therefore, my beloved brethren, let every man be swift to hear, slow to speak, slow to wrath; for the wrath of man does not produce the righteousness of God (James 1:19, 20).

Creating Love

ANXIOUS ABOUT CHILDREN'S SALVATION and need assurance:

Behold, children are a heritage from the LORD, the fruit of the womb is His reward (Psalm 127:3).

The righteous man walks in his integrity; his children are blessed after him (Proverbs 20:7).

Train up a child in the way he should go, and when he is old he will not depart from it (Proverbs 22:6).

For I will contend with him who contends with you, and I will save your children (Isaiah 49:25).

All your children shall be taught by the Lord, and great shall be the peace of your children (Isaiah 54:13).

CONFUSED and need guidance:

I will bless the LORD who has given me counsel; my heart also instructs me in the night seasons. I have set the LORD always before me; because He is at my right hand I shall not be moved (Psalm 16:7, 8).

I will instruct you and teach you in the way you should go: I will guide you with My eye (Psalm 32:8).

The steps of a good man are ordered by the LORD, and He delights in his way (Psalm 37:23).

You will guide me with Your counsel, and afterward receive me to glory (Psalm 73:24).

Your word is a lamp to my feet and a light to my path (Psalm 119:105).

Search me, O God, and know my heart; try me, and know my anxieties; and see if there is any wicked way in me, and lead me in the way everlasting (Psalm 139:23, 24).

In everything you do, put God first, and he will direct you and crown your efforts with success (Proverbs 3:6, TLB).

There is a way which seems right to a man, but its end is the way of death (Proverbs 14:12).

Listen to counsel and receive instruction, that you may be wise in your latter days. There are many plans in a man's heart, nevertheless the LORD'S counsel—that will stand (Proverbs 19:20, 21)

Through wisdom a house is built, and by understanding it is established; by knowledge the rooms are filled with all precious and pleasant riches (Proverbs 24:3, 4).

Fear God and keep His commandments, for this is the whole duty of man. For God will bring every work into judgment, including every secret thing, whether it is good or whether it is evil. (Ecclesiastes 11:13, 14).

I will bring the blind by a way they did not know; I will lead them in paths they have not known. I will make darkness light before them, and crooked places straight. These things I will do for them, and not forsake them (Isaiah 42:16).

The LORD will guide you continually, and satisfy your soul in drought, and strengthen your bones; you shall be like a watered garden, and like a spring of water, whose waters do not fail (Isaiah 58:11).

"I know the plans I have for you," says the Lord. "They are plans for good and not for evil, to give you a future and a hope. In those days when you pray, I will listen. You will find me when you seek me, if you look for me in earnest" (Jeremiah 29:11, TLB).

He has shown you, O man, what is good; and what does the LORD require of you but to do justly, to love mercy, and to walk humbly with your God? (Micah 6:8).

Don't look to the past and become discouraged. Push ahead and look to the future. Be strong and courageous and do the work that needs to be done . . . (Haggai 2:4 from a paraphrase, The Clear Word Bible).

DESPERATE and need help immediately:
It is time for You to act, O LORD (Psalm 119:126).

I cry out with my whole heart; hear me, O LORD! I will keep Your statutes. I cry out to You; save me, and I will keep Your testimonies. I rise before the dawning of the morning, and cry for help; I hope in Your word. My eyes are awake through the night watches, that I may meditate on Your word. Hear my voice according to Your lovingkindness; O LORD, revive me according to Your justice (Psalm 119:145-149).

DEPRESSED and need uplifting:
In my distress I called upon the LORD, and cried out to my God; He heard my voice from His temple, and my cry came before Him, even to His ears (Psalm 18:6).

You have also given me the shield of Your salvation; Your right hand has held me up, Your gentleness has made me great. You enlarged my path under me; So that my feet did not slip (Psalm 18:35, 36).

I am radiant with joy because of your mercy, for you have listened to my troubles and have seen the crisis in my soul. You have not handed me over to my enemy, but have given me open ground in which to maneuver (Psalm 31:7, 8, TLB).

O LORD, do not rebuke me in Your wrath, nor chasten me in Your hot displeasure! For Your arrows pierce me deeply, and Your hand presses me down. There is no soundness in my flesh because of Your anger, nor is there any health in my bones because of my sin. For my iniquities have gone over my head; like a heavy burden they are too heavy for me. My wounds are foul and festering because of my foolishness. I am troubled, I am bowed down greatly; I go mourning all the day long. For my loins are full of inflammation, and there is no soundness in my flesh. I am feeble and severely broken; I groan because of the turmoil of my heart. Lord, all my desire is before You; And my sighing is not hidden from You, My heart pants, my strength fails me; as for the light of my eyes, it also has gone from me. My loved ones and my friends stand aloof from my plague, and my kinsmen stand afar off. Those also who seek my life lay snares for me; those who seek my hurt speak of destruction, and plan deception all the day long. But I, like a deaf man, do not hear; And I am like a mute who does not open his mouth. Thus I am like a man who does not hear, and in whose mouth is no response. For in You, O LORD, I hope; You will hear, O Lord my God. . . . Do not forsake me, O LORD; O my God, be not far from me! Make haste to help me, O Lord, my salvation! (Psalm 38:1-15; 21, 22).

Why are you cast down, O my soul? And why are you disquieted within me? Hope in God; for I shall yet praise Him, the help of my countenance and my God (Psalm 42:11).

Then they cried out to the LORD in their trouble, and He delivered them out of their distresses. And He led them forth by the right way, that they might go to a city for habitation. O, that men would give thanks to the LORD for His goodness, and for His wonderful works to the children of men! For He satisfies the longing soul, and fills the hungry soul with goodness (Psalm 107:6-9).

Then they cry out to the LORD in their trouble, and He brings them out of their distresses. He calms the storm, so that its waves are still. Then they are glad because they are quiet; so He guides them to their desired haven. Oh, that men would give thanks to the LORD for His goodness, and for His wonderful works to the children of men! (Psalm 107:28-31).

Love-Cup Fillers From God's Word

Call to Me, and I will answer you, and show you great and mighty things, which you do not know (Jeremiah 33:3).

But the fruit of the Spirit is love, joy, peace, longsuffering, kindness, goodness, faithfulness, gentleness, self-control. Against such there is no law (Galatians 5:22, 23).

Finally, brethren, whatever things are true, whatever things are noble, whatever things are just, whatever things are pure, whatever things are lovely, whatever things are of good report, if there is any virtue and if there is anything praiseworthy—meditate on these things (Philippians 4:8).

DISCOURAGED and need hope:

Have I not commanded you? Be strong and of good courage; do not be afraid, nor be dismayed, for the Lord your God is with you wherever you go (Joshua 1:9).

He shall deliver you in six troubles, yes, in seven no evil shall touch you. In famine He shall redeem you from death, and in war from the power of the sword. You shall be hidden from the scourge of the tongue and of destruction when it comes. You shall laugh at destruction and famine, and you shall not be afraid of the beasts of the earth (Job 5:19-22).

Blessed is the man who walks not in the counsel of the ungodly, nor stands in the path of sinners, nor sits in the seat of the scornful; but his delight is in the law of the LORD, and in His law he meditates day and night. He shall be like a tree planted by the rivers of water, that brings forth its fruit in its season, whose leaf also shall not wither; and whatever he does shall prosper (Psalm 1:1-3).

Though he fall, he shall not be utterly cast down; for the LORD upholds him with His hand (Psalm 37:24).

Uphold me according to Your word, that I may live; and do not let me be ashamed of my hope (Psalm 119:116).

If it had not been the LORD who was on our side, when men rose up against us, then they would have swallowed us alive, when their wrath was kindled against us; then the waters would have overwhelmed us, the stream would have gone over our soul; then the swollen waters would have gone over our soul. Blessed be the LORD, who has not given us as prey to their teeth. Our soul has escaped as a bird from the snare of the fowlers; the snare is broken and we have escaped. Our help is in the name of the LORD, who made heaven and earth (Psalm 124:2-8).

Hope deferred makes the heart sick, but when the desire comes, it is a tree of life (Proverbs 13:12).

Creating Love

Yet there is one ray of hope: his compassion never ends. It is only the Lord's mercies that have kept us from complete destruction. Great is his faithfulness; his lovingkindness begins afresh each day. My soul claims the Lord as my inheritance; therefore I will hope in him. The Lord is wonderfully good to those who wait for him, to those who seek for him. It is good both to hope and wait quietly for the salvation of the Lord (Lamentations 3:21-25, TLB).

Let not your heart be troubled; you believe in God, believe also in Me. In My Father's house are many mansions; if it were not so, I would have told you. I go to prepare a place for you. And if I go and prepare a place for you, I will come again and receive you to Myself; that where I am there you may be also (John 14:1-3).

I know how to be abased, and I know how to abound. Everywhere and in all things I have learned both to be full and to be hungry, both to abound and to suffer need. I can do all things through Christ who strengthens me (Philippians 4:12, 13).

DOUBTFUL and need faith:

Is there anything too hard for the Lord? (Genesis 18:14, read circumstances around this text!)

What I want from you is your true thanks; I want your promises fulfilled. I want you to trust me in your times of trouble, so I can rescue you, and you can give me glory (Psalm 50:14, 15, TLB).

Make haste, O God, to deliver me! Make haste to help me, O LORD! Let them be ashamed and confounded who seek my life; Let them be turned back and confused who desire my hurt. (Psalm 70:1, 2)

I called on the LORD in distress; the LORD answered me and set me in a broad place. The LORD is on my side; I will not fear. What can man do to me? . . . It is better to trust in the LORD than to put confidence in man. It is better to trust in the LORD than to put confidence in princes (Psalm 118:5-9).

It shall come to pass that before they call, I will answer, and while they are still speaking, I will hear (Isaiah 65:24).

Ah, Lord God! Behold, You have made the heavens and the earth by Your great power and outstretched arm. There is nothing too hard for You (Jeremiah 32:17).

Call to Me, and I will answer you, and show you great and mighty things, which you do not know (Jeremiah 33:3).

Ask, and it will be given to you; seek and you will find; knock, and it will be opened to you. For everyone who asks receives, and he who seeks finds, and to him who knocks it will be opened (Matthew 7:7, 8).

"I say unto you, if you have faith as a mustard seed, you will say to this mountain, 'Move from here to there,' and it will move; and nothing will be impossible for you. However, this kind does not go out except by prayer and fasting" (Matthew 17:20, 21)

So Jesus answered and said to them, "Assuredly, I say to you, if you have faith and do not doubt, you will not only do what was done to the fig tree, but also if you say to this mountain, 'Be removed and be cast into the sea,' it will be done. And all things, whatever you ask in prayer, believing, you will receive (Matthew 21:21, 22)

"Most assuredly, I say to you, he who believes in Me, the works that I do he will do also; and greater works than these he will do, because I go to My Father. And whatever you ask in My name, that I will do, that the Father may be glorified in the Son. If you ask anything in My name, I will do it" (John 14:12-14).

"If you abide in Me, and My words abide in you, you will ask what you desire, and it shall be done for you. By this My Father is glorified, that you bear much fruit; so you will be My disciples" (John 15:7, 8).

Now to Him who is able to do exceedingly abundantly above all that we ask or think, according to the power that works in us, to Him be glory in the church by Christ Jesus throughout all ages, world without end. Amen (Ephesians 3:20, 21).

FEARFUL and need security:

Behold, I am with you and will keep you wherever you go, and will bring you back to this land; for I will not leave you until I have done what I have spoken to you (Genesis 28:15).

And when the servant of the man of God arose early and went out, there was an army, surrounding the city with horses and chariots. And his servant said to him, "Alas, my master! What shall we do?" So he answered, "Do not fear, for those who are with us are more than those who are with them." And Elisha prayed, and said, "LORD, I pray, open his eyes that he may see." Then the LORD opened the eyes of the young man, and he saw. And behold, the mountain was full of horses and chariots of fire all around Elisha (2 Kings 6:15-17).

If you would prepare your heart, And stretch out your hands toward Him; if iniquity were in your hand, and you put it far away, and would not let wickedness dwell in your tents; then surely you could lift up your face without spot; yes, you could be steadfast, and not fear; because you would forget your misery, and remember it as waters that have passed away, and your life would be brighter than noonday. Though you were dark, you would be like the morning. And you would be secure, because there is hope; yes, you would dig about you, and take your rest in safety. You would also lie down, and no one would make you afraid; yes, many would court your favor. But the eyes of the wicked will fail, and they shall not escape, and their hope—loss of life! (Job 11:13-20).

I lay down and slept; I awoke, for the LORD sustained me. I will not be afraid of ten thousands of people who have set themselves against me all around (Psalm 3:5, 6).

I will both lie down in peace, and sleep; for You alone, O LORD, make me dwell in safety (Psalm 4:8).

The LORD is my light and my salvation; whom shall I fear? The LORD is the strength of my life; of whom shall I be afraid? (Psalm 27:1).

You are my hiding place; You shall preserve me from trouble; You shall surround me with songs of deliverance (Psalm 32:7).

The angel of the LORD encamps all around those who fear Him, and delivers them (Psalm 34:7).

The righteous cry out, and the Lord hears, and delivers them out of all their troubles (Psalm 34:17).

God is our refuge and strength, a very present help in trouble. Therefore we will not fear, though the earth be removed, and though the mountains be carried into the midst of the sea (Psalm 46:1, 2).

He who dwells in the secret place of the Most High shall abide under the shadow of the Almighty. I will say of the LORD, "He is my refuge and my fortress; My God, in Him I will trust." Surely He shall deliver you from the snare of the fowler and from the perilous pestilence. He shall cover you with His feathers, And under His wings you shall take refuge; His truth shall be your shield and buckler. You shall not be afraid of the terror by night, nor of the arrow that flies by day, nor of the pestilence that walks in darkness, nor of the destruction that lays waste at noonday. A thousand may fall at your side, and ten thousand at your right hand; but it shall not come near you. Only with your eyes shall you look, and see the reward of the wicked. Because you have made the LORD, who is my refuge, even the Most High, your habitation, no evil shall befall you, nor shall any plague come near your dwelling; for He shall give His angels charge over you, to keep you in all your ways. They shall bear you up in their hands, lest you dash your foot against a stone. You shall tread upon the lion and the cobra, the young lion and the serpent you shall trample under foot. Because he has set his love upon Me, therefore I will deliver him; I will set him on high, because he has known My name. He shall call upon Me, and I will answer him; I will be with him in trouble; I will deliver him and honor him. With long life I will satisfy him, And show him My salvation (Psalm 91:1-16).

He will not be afraid of evil tidings; his heart is steadfast, trusting in the Lord (Psalm 112:7).

The LORD shall preserve you from all evil; He shall preserve your soul. The LORD shall preserve your going out and your coming in From this time forth, and even forevermore (Psalm 121:7, 8).

But whoever listens to me will dwell safely, and will be secure, without fear of evil (Proverbs 1:33).

He who heeds the word wisely will find good, and whoever trusts in the Lord, happy is he (Proverbs 16:20).

The name of the Lord is a strong tower; the righteous run to it and are safe (Proverbs 18:10).

Fear not, for I am with you; be not dismayed, for I am your God. I will strengthen you, yes, I will help you, I will uphold you with My righteous right hand (Isaiah 41:10).

For I, the LORD your God, will hold your right hand, saying to you, "Fear not, I will help you" (Isaiah 41:13).

When you pass through the waters, I will be with you; and through the rivers, they shall not overflow you. When you walk through the fire you shall not be burned, nor shall the flame scorch you. For I am the LORD your God. . . . (Isaiah 43:2, 3).

"Are not two sparrows sold for a copper coin? And not one of them falls to the ground apart from your Father's will. But the very hairs of your head are all numbered. Do not fear therefore; you are of more value than many sparrows" (Matthew 10:29-31).

But He said to them, "Why are you so fearful? How is it that you have no faith?" (Mark 4:40).

Creating Love

What then shall we say to these things? If God is for us, who can be against us? He who did not spare His own Son, but delivered Him up for us all, how shall He not with Him also freely give us all things? (Romans 8:31, 32).

For God has not given us a spirit of fear, but of power and of love and of a sound mind (2 Timothy 1:7).

So we may boldly say: "The LORD is my helper; I will not fear. What can man do to me?" (Hebrews 13:6).

And who is he who will harm you if you become followers of what is good? But even if you should suffer for righteousness' sake you are blessed. "And do not be afraid of their threats, nor be troubled" (1 Peter 3:13, 14).

FINANCIALLY WORRIED and need reassurance
(Also see WORRIED)

Because the Lord is my Shepherd, I have everything I need! He lets me rest in the meadow grass and leads me beside the quiet streams. He restores my failing health. He helps me do what honors him the most. Even when walking through the dark valley of death I will not be afraid, for you are close beside me, guarding, guiding all the way. You provide delicious foods for me in the presence of my enemies. You have welcomed me as your guest; blessings overflow! Your goodness and unfailing kindness shall be with me all of my life, and afterwards I will live with you forever in your home (Psalm 23, TLB).

Oh, fear the LORD, you His saints! There is no want to those who fear Him. The young lions lack and suffer hunger; but those who seek the LORD shall not lack any good thing (Psalm 34:9, 10).

The LORD knows the days of the upright, and their inheritance shall be forever. They shall not be ashamed in the evil time, and in the days of famine they shall be satisfied (Psalm 37:18, 19).

Yes, the LORD will give what is good; and our land will yield its increase. Righteousness will go before Him, and shall make His footsteps our pathway (Psalm 85:12, 13).

May the LORD give you increase more and more, you and your children. May you be blessed by the LORD, who made heaven and earth (Psalm 115:14, 15).

There is one who makes himself rich, yet has nothing; and one who makes himself poor, yet has great riches (Proverbs 13:7).

Wealth gained by dishonesty will be diminished, but he who gathers by labor will increase (Proverbs 13:11).

A good name is to be chosen rather than great riches, loving favor rather than silver and gold (Proverbs 22:1).

Better is a handful with quietness than both hands full, together with toil and grasping for the wind (Ecclesiastes 4:6).

Cast your bread upon the waters, for you will find it after many days (Ecclesiastes 11:1).

In the morning sow your seed, and in the evening do not withhold your hand; for you do not know which will prosper, either this or that, or whether both alike will be good (Ecclesiastes 11:6).

He will dwell on high; his place of defense will be the fortress of rocks; bread will be given him, his water will be sure (Isaiah 33:16).

When the poor and needy seek water, and there is none, and their tongues fail for thirst, I, the LORD, will hear them; I, the God of Israel, will not forsake them. I will open rivers in desolate heights, and fountains in the midst of the valleys; I will make the wilderness a pool of water, and the dry land springs of water . . . that they may see and know, and consider and understand together, that the hand of the LORD has done this, and the Holy One of Israel has created it (Isaiah 41:17, 18, 20).

"Will a man rob God? Yet you have robbed Me! But you say, 'In what way have we robbed You?' In tithes and offerings. . . . Bring all the tithes into the storehouse, that there may be food in My house, and prove Me now in this," says the Lord of hosts, "if I will not open for you the windows of heaven and pour out for you such blessing that there will not be room enough to receive it (Malachi 3:8,10).

For your Father knows the things you have need of before you ask Him (Matthew 6:8b).

Do not lay up for yourselves treasures on earth, where moth and rust destroy and where thieves break in and steal; but lay up for yourselves treasures in heaven, where neither moth nor rust destroys and where thieves do not break in and steal. For where your treasure is, there your heart will be also (Matthew 6:19-21).

And He said to His disciples, "Therefore I say to you, do not worry about your life, what you will eat or what you will drink; nor about your body, what you will put on. Is not life more than food, and the body more than clothing? Look at the birds of the air, for they neither sow nor reap, nor gather into barns; yet your heavenly Father feeds them. Are you not of more value than they? Which of you by worrying can add one cubit to his stature? So why do you worry about clothing? Consider the lilies of the field, how they grow: they neither toil nor spin; and yet I say to you that even Solomon in all his glory was not arrayed like one of these. Now if God so clothes the grass of the field, which today is, and tomorrow is thrown into the oven, will He not much more clothe you, O you of little faith? Therefore do not worry, saying 'What shall we eat?' or 'What shall we drink?' or 'What shall we wear?' For after all these things the Gentiles seek. For your heavenly Father knows that you need all these things. But seek first the kingdom of God and His righteousness, and all these things shall be added to you. Therefore do not worry about tomorrow, for tomorrow will worry about its own things. Sufficient for the day is its own trouble" (Matthew 6:25-34).

Every day has enough trouble of its own. Live one day at a time (Matthew 6:34).

For we brought nothing into this world, and it is certain we can carry nothing out. And having food and clothing, with these we shall be content (1 Timothy 6:7, 8).

You do not have because you do not ask. You ask and do not receive, because you ask amiss, that you may spend it on your pleasures (James 4:2, 3).

Beloved, I pray that you may prosper in all things and be in health, just as your soul prospers (3 John 2).

GUILTY and need forgiveness:

If My people who are called by My name will humble themselves, and pray and seek My face, and turn from their wicked ways, then I will hear from heaven, and will forgive their sin and heal their land (2 Chronicles 7:14).

Do not remember the sins of my youth, nor my transgressions: According to Your mercy remember me, for Your goodness' sake, O LORD. Good and upright is the LORD; therefore He teaches sinners in the way. The humble He guides in justice, and the humble He teaches His way. All the paths of the LORD are mercy and truth, to such as keep His covenant and His testimonies. For Your name's sake, O LORD, pardon my iniquity, for it is great (Psalm 25:7-11).

Create in me a clean heart, O God, and renew a steadfast spirit within me. Do not cast me away from Your presence, and do not take Your Holy Spirit from me

Love-Cup Fillers From God's Word

(Psalm 51:10, 11).

For You, Lord, are good, and ready to forgive, and abundant in mercy to all those who call upon You (Psalm 86:5).

As far as the east is from the west, so far has He removed our transgressions from us (Psalm 103:12).

"Come now, and let us reason together," Says the LORD, "though your sins are like scarlet, they shall be as white as snow; though they are red like crimson, they shall be as wool" (Isaiah 1:18).

I, even I, am He who blots out your transgressions for My own sake; And I will not remember your sins (Isaiah 43:25).

I have blotted out, like a thick cloud, your transgressions, And like a cloud, your sins. Return to Me, for I have redeemed you (Isaiah 44:22).

Let the wicked forsake his way, and the unrighteous man his thoughts; let him return to the LORD, and He will have mercy on him; and to our God, for He will abundantly pardon (Isaiah 55:7).

"For I will forgive their iniquity, and their sin I will remember no more"(Jeremiah 31:34).

He will again have compassion on us, and will subdue our iniquities. You will cast all our sins into the depths of the sea (Micah 7:19).

Forgive, and you will be forgiven (Luke 6:37b).

In Him we have redemption through His blood, the forgiveness of sins, according to the riches of His grace which He made to abound toward us in all wisdom and prudence (Ephesians 1:7, 8).

"For I will be merciful to their unrighteousness, and their sins and their lawless deeds I will remember no more" (Hebrews 8:12).

If we confess our sins, He is faithful and just to forgive us our sins and to cleanse us from all unrighteousness (1 John 1:9).

IMPATIENT or FRUSTRATED and need patience?

Wait on the Lord; Be of good courage, and He shall strengthen your heart; wait, I say, on the Lord! (Psalm 27:14).

Rest in the Lord and wait patiently for Him; do not fret because of him who prospers in his way, because of the man who brings wicked schemes to pass. . . . For evildoers shall be cut off; but those who wait on the Lord, they shall inherit the earth (Psalm 37:7, 9).

I waited patiently for the Lord; and He inclined to me, and heard my cry. He also brought me up out of a horrible pit, out of the miry clay, and set my feet upon a rock, and established my steps. He has put a new song in my mouth—Praise to our God; many will see it and fear, and will trust in the Lord (Psalm 40:1-3).

To everything there is a season, a time for every purpose under heaven (Ecclesiastes 3:1).

Dear brothers, is your life full of difficulties and temptations? Then be happy, for when the way is rough, your patience has a chance to grow. So let it grow, and don't try to squirm out of your problems. For when your patience is finally in full bloom, then you will be ready for anything, strong in character, full and complete (James 1:1-3, TLB).

INSULTED or HURT and need to forgive:

If your enemy is hungry, give him food! If he is thirsty, give him something to drink! This will make him feel ashamed of himself, and God will reward you (Proverbs 25:21, 22, TLB).

Blessed are those who are persecuted for righteousness' sake, for theirs is the kingdom of heaven. Blessed are you when they revile and persecute you, and say all kinds of evil against you falsely for My sake. Rejoice and be exceedingly glad, for great is your reward in heaven, for so they persecuted the prophets who were before you (Matthew 5:10-12).

But I say to you, love your enemies, bless those who curse you, do good to those who hate you, and pray for those who spitefully use you and persecute you, that you may be sons of your Father in heaven; for He makes His sun rise on the evil and on the good, and sends rain on the just and on the unjust (Matthew 5:44, 45)

Moreover if your brother sins against you, go and tell him his fault between you and him alone. If he hears you, you have gained your brother (Matthew 18:15).

Take heed to yourselves. If your brother sins against you, rebuke him; and if he repents, forgive him. And if he sins against you seven times in a day, and seven times in a day returns to you, saying, "I repent," you shall forgive him (Luke 17:3, 4)

And be kind to one another, tenderhearted, forgiving one another, just as God in Christ also forgave you (Ephesians 4:32).

JEALOUS or ENVIOUS and need to accept:
Do not be afraid when one becomes rich, when the glory of his house is increased; for when he dies he shall carry nothing away; his glory shall not descend after him (Psalm 49:16, 17).

A sound heart is life to the body But envy is rottenness to the bones (Proverbs 14:30).

Pride goes before destruction, and a haughty spirit before a fall. Better to be of a humble spirit with the lowly, than to divide the spoil with the proud (Proverbs 16:18, 19).

Let everyone be sure that he is doing his very best, for then he will have the personal satisfaction of work well done, and won't need to compare himself with someone else. Each of us must bear some faults and burdens of his own. For none of us is perfect! (Galatians 6:4, 5, TLB).

But if you have bitter envy and self-seeking in your hearts, do not boast and lie against the truth. This wisdom does not descend from above, but is earthly, sensual, demonic. For where envy and self-seeking exist, confusion and every evil thing will be there (James 3:14-16).

And above all things have fervent love for one another, for "love will cover a multitude of sins." Be hospitable to one another without grumbling. As each one has received a gift, minister it to one another, as good stewards of the manifold grace of God (1 Peter 4:8-10).

There is no fear in love; but perfect love casts out fear, because fear involves torment. But he who fears has not been made perfect in love. We love Him because He first loved us (1 John 4:17-19).

LONELY and need friendship and support:
I will not leave you nor forsake you (Joshua 1:5b).

I am a companion of all those who fear You, and of those who keep Your precepts (Psalm 119:63).

Where can I go from Your Spirit? Or where can I flee from Your presence? If I ascend into heaven, You are there; if I make my bed in hell, behold, You are there. If I take the wings of the morning, and dwell in the uttermost parts of the sea, even there Your hand shall lead me, and Your right hand shall hold me (Psalm 139:7-10).

For the mountains shall depart and the hills be removed, but My kindness shall not depart from you, nor shall My covenant of peace be removed," says the LORD, who has mercy on you (Isaiah 54:10).

"Lo, I am with you always, even to the end of the age" (Matthew 28:20).

"If you love Me, keep My commandments. And I will pray the Father, and He will give you another Helper, that He may abide with you forever, even the Spirit of truth, whom the world cannot receive, because it neither sees Him nor knows Him; but you know Him, for He dwells with you and will be in you. I will not leave you orphans: I will come to you" (John 14:15-18).

Draw near to God and He will draw near to you (James 4:8a).

"Behold, I stand at the door and knock. If anyone hears My voice and opens the door, I will come in to him and dine with him, and he with Me" (Revelation 3:20).

MOURNFUL and need comfort:

The Lord is near to those who have a broken heart, and saves such as have a contrite spirit (Psalm 34:18).

You number my wanderings; put my tears into Your bottle; are they not in Your book? When I cry out to You, then my enemies will turn back; this I know, because God is for me (Psalm 56:8, 9).

For You have delivered my soul from death, my eyes from tears, and my feet from falling. I will walk before the LORD in the land of the living. (Psalm 116:8, 9).

Those who sow in tears shall reap in joy. He who continually goes forth weeping, bearing seed for sowing, shall doubtless come again with rejoicing, bringing his sheaves with him (Psalm 126:5-6).

He heals the broken-hearted and binds up their wounds (Psalm 147:3).

He will swallow up death forever, and the Lord GOD will wipe away tears from all faces; the rebuke of His people He will take away from all the earth; for the LORD has spoken. And it will be said in that day: "Behold, this is our

God; we have waited for Him, and He will save us. This is the LORD; we have waited for Him; we will be glad and rejoice in His Salvation" (Isaiah 25:8, 9).

Blessed are those who mourn, for they shall be comforted (Matthew 5:4).

Behold, I tell you a mystery: We shall not all sleep, but we shall all be changed—in a moment, in the twinkling of an eye, at the last trumpet. For the trumpet will sound, and the dead will be raised incorruptible, and we shall be changed. . . . Then shall be brought to pass the saying that is written: "Death is swallowed up in victory. O Death, where is your sting? O Hades, where is your victory?" (1 Corinthians 15:51-55).

Blessed by the God and Father of our Lord Jesus Christ, the Father of mercies and God of all comfort, who comforts us in all our tribulation, that we may be able to comfort those who are in any trouble, with the comfort with which we ourselves are comforted by God (2 Corinthians 1:3, 4).

They shall neither hunger anymore nor thirst anymore; the sun shall not strike them, nor any heat; for the Lamb who is in the midst of the throne will shepherd them and lead them to living fountains of waters. And God will wipe away every tear from their eyes (Revelation 7:16, 17).

REJECTED and need acceptance and love:
The LORD has appeared of old to me, saying: "Yes, I have loved you with an everlasting love; therefore with lovingkindness I have drawn you (Jeremiah 31:3).

I drew them with gentle cords, with bands of love, and I was to them as those who take the yoke from their neck. I stooped and fed them. (Hosea 11:4).

The LORD your God is with you, he is mighty to save. He will take great delight in you, he will quiet you with his love, he will rejoice over you with singing (Zephaniah 3:17, NIV).

For God so loved the world that He gave His only begotten Son, that whoever believes in Him should not perish but have everlasting life (John 3:16).

For I am persuaded that neither death nor life; nor angels nor principalities nor powers, nor things present nor things to come, nor height nor depth, nor any other created thing, shall be able to separate us from the love of God which is in Christ Jesus our Lord (Romans 8:38, 39).

May your roots go down deep into the soil of God's marvelous love; and may you be able to feel and understand, as all God's children should, how long, how wide, how deep, and how high his love really is; and to experience this love for yourselves, though it is so great that you will never see the end of it or fully know or understand it. And so at last you will be filled up with God himself (Ephesians 3:17, 19, TLB).

By this we know love, because He laid down His life for us. And we also ought to lay down our lives for the brethren. But whoever has this world's goods, and sees his brother in need, and shuts up his heart from him, how does the love of God abide in him? My little children, let us not love in word or in tongue, but in deed and in truth (1 John 3:16-18).

SICK and need healing:
So you shall serve the LORD your God, and He will bless your bread and your water. And I will take sickness away from the midst of you (Exodus 23:25).

But know that the LORD has set apart for Himself him who is godly; the LORD will hear when I call to Him (Psalm 4:3).

Bless the LORD, O my soul, and forget not all His benefits: who forgives all your iniquities, who heals all your diseases, who redeems your life from destruction, who crowns you with lovingkindness and tender mercies, who satisfies your mouth with good things, so that your youth is renewed like the eagle's (Psalm 103:2-5).

Pleasant words are like a honeycomb, sweetness to the soul and health to the bones (Proverbs 16:24).

A merry heart does good, like medicine, but a broken spirit dries the bones (Proverbs 17:22).

I have seen his ways, and will heal him; I will also lead him, and restore comforts to him. . . . Peace, peace to him who is far off and to him who is near," Says the LORD, "and I will heal him" (Isaiah 57:18, 19).

"Then your light shall break forth like the morning, your healing shall spring forth speedily, and your righteousness shall go before you; the glory of the LORD shall be your rear guard. Then you shall call, and the LORD will answer; you shall cry, and He will say, 'Here I am' " (Isaiah 58:8, 9).

"For I will restore health to you and heal you of your wounds" (Jeremiah 30:17a).

Jesus said to him, "If you can believe, all things are possible to him who believes" (Mark 9:23).

Therefore we do not lose heart. Even though our outward man is perishing, yet the inward man is being renewed day by day. For our light affliction, which is but for a moment, is working for us a far more exceeding and eternal weight of glory, while we do not look at the things which are seen, but at the things which are not seen. For the things which are seen are temporary, but the things which are not seen are eternal (2 Corinthians 4:16-18).

And He said to me, "My grace is sufficient for you, for My strength is made perfect in weakness." Therefore most gladly I will rather boast in my infirmities, that the power of Christ may rest upon me. Therefore I take pleasure in infirmities, in reproaches, in needs, in persecutions, in distresses, for Christ's sake. For when I am weak, then I am strong (2 Corinthians 12:9, 10).

Is anyone among you sick? Let him call for the elders of the church, and let them pray over him, anointing him with oil in the name of the Lord. And the prayer of faith will save the sick, and the Lord will raise him up (James 5:14, 15).

But may the God of all grace, who called us to His eternal glory by Christ Jesus, after you have suffered a while, perfect, establish, strengthen, and settle you (1 Peter 5:10).

SORROWFUL and need joy:
Sing praise to the LORD, you saints of His, and give thanks at the remembrance of His holy name. For His anger is but for a moment, His favor is for life; weeping may endure for a night, but joy comes in the morning" (Psalm 30:4, 5).

O come, let us sing unto the LORD! Let us shout joyfully to the Rock of our salvation. Let us come before His presence with thanksgiving; let us shout joyfully to Him with psalms. For the LORD is the great God, and the great King above all gods (Psalm 95:1-3).

The LORD has done great things for us, whereof we are glad (Psalm 126:3).

For God gives wisdom and knowledge and joy to a man who is good in His sight (Ecclesiastes 2:26a).

For you shall go out with joy, and be led out with peace; the mountains and the hills shall break forth into singing before you, and all the trees of the field shall clap their hands (Isaiah 55:12).

Creating Love

Though the fig tree may not blossom, nor fruit be on the vines; though the labor of the olive may fail, and the fields yield no food; though the flock be cut off from the fold, and there be no herd in the stalls—yet I will rejoice in the LORD, I will joy in the God of my salvation (Habakkuk 3:17, 18).

"As the Father loved Me, I also have loved you; abide in My love. If you keep My commandments, you will abide in My love, just as I have kept My Father's commandments and abide in His love. These things I have spoken to you, that My joy may remain in you, and that your joy may be full" (John 15:9-11).

"Most assuredly, I say to you that you will weep and lament, but the world will rejoice; and you will be sorrowful, but your sorrow will be turned into joy. A woman, when she is in labor, has sorrow because her hour has come; but as soon as she has given birth to the child, she no longer remembers the anguish, for joy that a human being has been born into the world. Therefore you now have sorrow; but I will see you again and your heart will rejoice, and your joy no one will take from you" (John 16:20-22).

Rejoice in the Lord always. Again I will say, rejoice! (Philippians 4:4).

Beloved, do not think it strange concerning the fiery trial which is to try you, as though some strange thing happened to you; but rejoice to the extent that you partake of Christ's sufferings, that when His glory is revealed, you may also be glad with exceeding joy (1 Peter 5:12).

TEMPTED and need strength:

Who can understand his errors? Cleanse me from secret faults. Keep back Your servant also from presumptuous sins; let them not have dominion over me. Then I shall be blameless, and I shall be innocent of great transgression (Psalm 19:12, 13).

Cast your burden on the LORD, and He shall sustain you; He shall never permit the righteous to be moved (Psalm 55:22).

Turn away my eyes from looking at worthless things, and revive me in Your way (Psalm 119:37).

My help comes from the LORD, who made heaven and earth. He will not allow your foot to be moved; He who keeps you will not slumber. Behold, He who keeps Israel shall neither slumber nor sleep (Psalm 121:2-4).

"Watch and pray, lest you enter into temptation. The spirit truly is ready, but the flesh is weak" (Mark 14:38).

No temptation has overtaken you except such as is common to man; but God is faithful, who will not allow you to be tempted beyond what you are able, but with the temptation will also make the way of escape, that you may be able to bear it (1 Corinthians 10:13).

For in that He Himself has suffered, being tempted, He is able to aid those who are tempted (Hebrews 2:18).

Blessed is the man who endures temptation; for when he has been proved, he will receive the crown of life which the Lord has promised to those who love Him (James 1:12).

Therefore submit to God. Resist the devil and he will flee from you. Draw near to God and He will draw near to you (James 4:7, 8).

The Lord knows how to deliver the godly out of temptations (2 Peter 2:9a).

TIRED and need rest and renewed vitality:
Remember the Sabbath day, to keep it holy. Six days you shall labor and do all your work, but the seventh day is the Sabbath of the LORD your God. In it you shall do no work; you, nor your son, nor your daughter, nor your manservant, nor your maidservant, nor your cattle, nor your stranger who is within your gates. For in six days the LORD made the heaven and the earth, the sea, and all that is in them, and rested the seventh day. Therefore the LORD blessed the Sabbath day and hallowed it (Exodus 20:8-11).

And He said, "My Presence will go with you, and I will give you rest" (Exodus 33:14).

I lay down and slept; I awoke, for the LORD sustained me (Psalm 3:5).

And I said, "Oh, that I had wings like a dove! For then I would fly away and be at rest. Indeed, I would wander far off, and remain in the wilderness" (Psalm 55:6, 7).

But those who wait on the LORD shall renew their strength; they shall mount up with wings like angels, they shall run and not be weary, they shall walk and not faint (Isaiah 40:31).

"Come to Me, all you who labor and are heavy laden, and I will give you rest. Take My yoke upon you and learn from Me, for I am gentle and lowly in heart, and you will find rest for your souls. For My yoke is easy and My burden is light (Matthew 11:28-30).

Creating Love

And He said to them, "Come aside by yourselves to a deserted place and rest a while." For there were many coming and going, and they did not even have time to eat (Mark 6:31).

TROUBLED and need peace:

Now acquaint yourself with Him, and be at peace; thereby good will come to you (Job 22:21).

The LORD will give strength to His people; the LORD will bless His people with peace (Psalm 29:11).

Great peace have those who love Your law, and nothing causes them to stumble (Psalm 119:165).

When you lie down, you will not be afraid; yes, you will lie down and your sleep will be sweet (Proverbs 3:24).

In the fear of the LORD there is strong confidence, and His children will have a place of refuge. The fear of the LORD is a fountain of life, to avoid the snares of death (Proverbs 14:26, 27).

You will keep him in perfect peace whose mind is stayed on You, because he trusts in You (Isaiah 26:3).

The work of righteousness will be peace, and the effect of righteousness, quietness and assurance forever. My people will dwell in a peaceful habitation, in secure dwellings, and in quiet resting places (Isaiah 32:17, 18).

"Peace I leave with you, My peace I give to you; not as the world gives do I give to you. Let not your heart be troubled, neither let it be afraid" (John 14:27).

"These things I have spoken to you, that in Me you may have peace. In the world you will have tribulation; but be of good cheer, I have overcome the world" (John 16:33).

For God is not the author of confusion but of peace (1 Corinthians 14:33).

Be anxious for nothing, but in everything by prayer and supplication, with thanksgiving, let your requests be made known to God; and the peace of God, which surpasses all understanding, will guard your hearts and minds through Christ Jesus (Philippians 4:6, 7).

He who would love life and see good days, let him refrain his tongue from evil, and his lips from speaking guile; let him turn away from evil and do good; let him seek peace and pursue it. For the eyes of the LORD are on the righteous, and his ears are open to their prayers; but the face of the LORD is against those who do evil (1 Peter 3:10-12).

Grace and peace be multiplied to you in the knowledge of God and of Jesus our Lord (2 Peter 1:2).

UNDISCIPLINED and need determination:

Go to the ant, you sluggard! Consider her ways and be wise (Proverbs 6:6).

He who tills his land will be satisfied with bread, but he who follows frivolity is devoid of understanding (Proverbs 12:11).

Do you see a man who excels in his work? He will stand before kings (Proverbs 22:29).

Whatever your hand finds to do, do it with your might; for there is no work or device or knowledge or wisdom in the grave where you are going (Ecclesiastes 9:10).

Do you not know that those who run in a race all run, but one receives the prize? Run in such a way that you may obtain it. . . . Therefore I run thus: not with uncertainty. Thus I fight: not as one who beats the air. But I discipline my body and bring it into subjection, lest, when I have preached to others, I myself should become disqualified (1 Corinthians 9:24, 26, 27).

Not that I have already attained, or am already perfected; but I press on, that I may lay hold of that for which Christ Jesus has also laid hold of me. Brethren, I do not count myself to have apprehended; but one thing I do, forgetting those things which are behind and reaching forward to those things which are ahead, I press toward the goal for the prize of the upward call of God in Christ Jesus (Philippians 3:12-14).

And whatever you do, do it heartily, as to the Lord and not to men, knowing that from the Lord you will receive the reward of the inheritance; for you serve the Lord Christ (Colossians 3:23, 24).

WEAK and need strength:

Do not sorrow, for the joy of the LORD is your strength (Nehemiah 8:10b).

The LORD is my strength and my shield; my heart trusted in Him, and I am helped; therefore my heart greatly rejoices, and with my song I will praise Him (Psalm 28:7).

He gives power to the weak, and to those who have no might He increases strength. Even the youths shall faint and be weary, and the young men shall utterly fall, but those who wait on the LORD shall renew their strength; they shall mount up with wings like eagles, they shall run and not be weary, they shall walk and not faint (Isaiah 40:29-31).

The LORD God is my strength; He will make my feet like deer's feet, and He will make me walk on the high hills (Habakkuk 3:19).

I can do all things through Christ who strengthens me (Philippians 4:13).

WORRIED and need reassurance
(also see Financially Worried)

Cast your burden on the LORD, and He shall sustain you; He shall never permit the righteous to be moved (Psalm 55:22).

Blessed be the Lord, who daily loads us with benefits (Psalm 68:19).

For the LORD God is a sun and shield; the LORD will give grace and glory; no good thing will He withhold from those who walk uprightly. O LORD of hosts, blessed is the man who trusts in You! (Psalm 84: 11, 12).

Those who sow in tears shall reap in joy. He who continually goes forth weeping, bearing seed for sowing, Shall doubtless come again with rejoicing, bringing his sheaves with him (Psalm 126:5, 6).

You will keep him in perfect peace, whose mind is stayed on You, because he trusts in You. Trust in the Lord forever, for in YAH, the Lord is everlasting strength (Isaiah 26:3, 4).

"For My thoughts are not your thoughts, nor are your ways My ways," says the LORD. "For as the heavens are higher than the earth, so are My ways higher than your ways, and My thoughts than your thoughts. For as the rain comes down, and the snow from heaven, and do not return there, but water the earth, and make it bring forth and bud, that it may give seed to the sower and bread to the eater, so shall My word be that goes forth from My mouth; it shall not return to Me void, but it shall accomplish what I please, and it shall prosper in the thing for which I sent it" (Isaiah 55:8-11).

And we know that all things work together for good to those who love God, to those who are the called according to His purpose (Romans 8:28).

And my God shall supply all your need according to His riches in glory by

Christ Jesus (Philippians 4:19).

WORTHLESS and need personal value:

The LORD bless you and keep you; the LORD make His face shine upon you, and be gracious to you; the LORD lift up His countenance upon you, and give you peace (Numbers 6:24-26).

He shall call upon Me, and I will answer him; I will be with him in trouble; I will deliver him and honor him. With long life I will satisfy him, and show him My salvation (Psalm 91:15).

Do good, O LORD, to those who are good, and to those who are upright in their hearts (Psalm 125:4).

Blessed is every one who fears the LORD, who walks in His ways. When you eat the labor of your hands, you shall be happy, and it shall be well with you. Your wife shall be like a fruitful vine in the very heart of your house, your children like olive plants all around your table. Behold, thus shall the man be blessed who fears the LORD. The LORD bless you out of Zion, and may you see the good of Jerusalem all the days of your life. Yes, may you see your children's children (Psalm 128:1-6).

O LORD, You have searched me and known me. You know my sitting down and my rising up; You understand my thought afar off. You comprehend my path and my lying down, and are acquainted with all my ways. For there is not a word on my tongue, but behold, O LORD, You know it altogether. You have hedged me behind and before, and laid Your hand upon me. Such knowledge is too wonderful for me; it is high, I cannot attain it (Psalm 139:1-6).

For You have formed my inward parts; You have covered me in my mother's womb. I will praise You, for I am fearfully and wonderfully made; marvelous are Your works (Psalm 139:13, 14).

How precious also are Your thoughts to me, O God! How great is the sum of them! If I should count them, they would be more in number than the sand; when I awake I am still with You (Psalm 139:17, 18).

Many daughters have done well, but you excel them all. Charm is deceitful and beauty is vain, but a woman who fears the LORD, she shall be praised. Give her of the fruit of her hands, and let her own works praise her in the gates (Proverbs 31:29-31).

Creating Love

"Before I formed you in the womb I knew you; before you were born I sanctified you; and I ordained you a prophet to the nations" (Jeremiah 1:5).

For God so loved the world that He gave His only begotten Son, that whoever believes in Him should not perish but have everlasting life (John 3:16).

Therefore, as the elect of God, holy and beloved, put on tender mercies, kindness, humbleness of mind, meekness, longsuffering; bearing with one another, and forgiving one another, if anyone has a complaint against another; even as Christ forgave you, so you also must do. But above all these things put on love, which is the bond of perfection (Colossians 3:12-14).

But thanks be to God, who gives us the victory through our Lord Jesus Christ. Therefore, my beloved brethren, be steadfast, immovable, always abounding in the work of the Lord, knowing that your labor is not in vain in the Lord (1 Corinthians 15:57, 58).

Humble yourselves in the sight of the Lord, and He will lift you up (James 4:10).

Therefore humble yourselves under the mighty hand of God, that He may exalt you in due time, casting all your care upon Him, for He cares for you (1 Peter 5:6, 7).

Behold what manner of love the Father has bestowed on us, that we should be called children of God! (1 John 3:1a).